PENGUIN BOOKS

No Safe Place

Emily Christie has campaigned for justice for sexual abuse victims and gained the qualifications she was too traumatized to work for when she was at school. Now thirty-two, Emily still has physical injuries from her childhood, and is unable to work, but she is happy to be a stay-at-home mum with her beautiful daughter. She lives in Scotland.

No Safe Place

EMILY CHRISTIE

PENGUIN BOOKS

London Borough of Southwark

SK 2399982 9		
Askews & Holts	18-Apr-2014	
CHR HARD	£6.99	

Penguin
Penguin Grou   USA
                                                                             ada M4P 2Y3
Penguin Ire   ooks Ltd)
Penguin   ustralia
Penguin Books   10 017, India
Penguin   aland

Penguin Books Ltd, Registered Offices: 80 Strand, London WC2R ORL, England

www.penguin.com

First published 2010

2

Copyright © Emily Christie, 2010

The moral right of the author has been asserted

Set in Monotype Garamond
Printed in England by Clays Ltd, St Ives plc

978–0–141–04089–9

www.greenpenguin.co.uk

Penguin Books is committed to a sustainable future
for our business, our readers and our planet.
The book in your hands is made from paper
certified by the Forest Stewardship Council.

Contents

To my beautiful daughter – you are my heart, my soul and my inspiration. You give me the strength to help fight for the safety of future generations of children. I love you to the stars and back.

I'm In Control

The days, the weeks, the months, the years,
They all carry a brand new fear,
The fear to live a life of my own,
To take control and not be owned,
My fear of living life was overpowered,
When my heart was devoured,
And the bitter taste of each tear,
Would melt away my every fear.
So I let my heart open,
To deal with all the pain and hurt,
To feel my heart grow stronger,
And echo with each new breath,
So please won't you realize,
That I take back my own control,
That I am here.

Emily Christie

Prologue: Truth Heals

As the car slammed into me with a sickening thud, my head hit tarmac and everything dissolved into blackness. Then, through the fog of semi-consciousness, I heard an ambulance siren screaming in the distance. Even though help was on the way, my stomach tightened with terror. I tried to crawl away, but the shock of the car accident made it impossible.

One of my size two shoes lay forlornly in the road.

Terrifyingly, being knocked down was the least of my worries.

I looked up and the face of the ambulance driver loomed over me. He smiled a toothy, friendly grin, and I recoiled in horror. It was my grandad. He was a respected member of the community, someone who *saved* lives. But behind closed doors he was a vile pervert, a man who thought nothing of abusing me in the most degrading way possible. He had wrecked my life.

As he lifted me onto a stretcher, I was shaking. The crowd of people gathered round must have thought I was in shock from the accident. Grandad slid me into the ambulance, and the doors slammed shut behind us. I watched in despair as the last patch of blue sky disappeared. In the claustrophobic confines, his smell was overwhelming. It was a scent I associated with fear, pain and aloneness. Bending over to fix an oxygen mask over my face, his eyes bored into me. Then, in a sinister tone, he whispered in my ear, 'Don't tell anyone, it's our little secret.'

I was ten years old. I'd been playing happily outside the police station in a sleepy, picturesque village, where my dad – a police officer himself – lived. You'd imagine there wasn't a safer place in the world for a little girl to grow up. But without my parents knowing, I was being groomed, abused and brutalized by my grandad. I was a sexual plaything for him – I was his special little girl.

Many people didn't want me to tell this story. They wanted me to brush it under the carpet. 'It's over now, what's the point of talking about it?' they said to me. But it will *never* be over for me. This story is part of who I am, and not a second goes by when I'm not affected in some way by what happened. I can never forget, but I've found the strength to survive.

It takes a coward to abuse a defenceless child, but it takes courage for that child to tell the truth. Back then I was far too young and terrified to tell anyone what my grandad was doing to me. I was scared into silence. But I'm not frightened any more, and I *want* to speak out. He might have controlled me in the past, but this is my way of taking control back.

Silence allows child abuse to continue. By speaking out, by letting others know that they aren't alone, we can be strong together – and put a stop to it.

I always say that he picked the wrong girl when he

chose me. I refuse to be kept quiet. This is my story of living through ten years of horrific sexual abuse – and how I made the journey from victim to survivor.

1. Family Portrait

Overlooking a dramatic coastline, in a sleepy part of Scotland, my family lived in the kind of place most people dream of moving to. Watching seagulls wheeling in the sky, with waves splashing across my feet as I collected shells, Mum would tell me how lucky our family was.

At five, I was too young to understand what she meant, and took all the natural beauty on my doorstep for granted. Mum would ruffle my hair, then join me in my favourite game of wave-chasing, laughing as I squealed with delight.

It wasn't just our location we had to be thankful for. Our close-knit family was the backbone of the community, and we were respected by everyone in the area. Legend had it that our bloodline was descended from a famous clan – lords who had lived and ruled on one of Scotland's wild isolated islands. Dad liked to tell my older brother Tom and me about it, trying to make us proud of our heritage. 'I'm a king!' Tom would shout, jumping onto the sofa. 'Well, I'm a princess!' I would reply, swishing my long hair comically. We also had a baby brother, Richard, but he was too young to join in our games.

Mum would laugh the rumours off and say, 'Where's my castle then?'

Dad would shrug and gesture as if to say, 'Isn't this good enough?'

He was right; even though we lived in a modest home, we were very happy. Mum was a natural homemaker and the house always had a welcoming mix of fresh lemony scent and the delicious smell of home-baked cakes.

When local children grew up they never left the area – why would they? So generations lived close by, really involved in each other's lives. We were the same – lots of relatives lived nearby. My grandparents lived close to us, as did my great-granny Hobbs, a fierce old Scottish woman whom we often visited, and whom I loved dearly.

My dad's parents were a big part of our lives and we'd visit them every weekend, and Grandad would often pop round to visit on week nights.

Grandad was a paramedic and Dad was training to join the police force, so that was another thing in our favour. The men in our family were central characters in the community and wherever we went, people would give us cheery waves and say hello. I was proud to be a Christie, and I would often pronounce my surname with special emphasis, just to let people know who I was.

Mum was right, I was one of the luckiest girls in the world – even if I didn't realize it at the time.

Right from the start, Grandad had an extra special bond with me.

I was the first girl to be born into Dad's growing family, coming just over four years after my oldest brother, Tom. Grandad was ecstatic when Dad announced the baby was a little girl. When Tom had been born, Grandad had been happy for my parents, but not as thrilled as he seemed to be with my arrival.

Looking back, I see now that from the second I drew breath I was earmarked as his and he was a constant presence by my side.

Dad must have been thrilled by his father's interest in me – everyone wants to make their parents proud. He was in his dad's good books, and that made him happy. He had no reason to suspect an ulterior motive.

My parents loved my brother very much, but having a girl in the family was a breath of fresh air for everyone. I bloomed with all the attention, becoming a girly girl who loved to be at the centre of things. As soon as I could speak it became obvious I had a talent for singing, and there was nothing I loved more than dressing up and putting on a performance for everyone. Grandad, along with everyone else, clapped with glee to see me dancing around like a ball of positive energy.

I was just what the family needed.

For Mum, it must have been a welcome relief to have some female company – even if I was far too young to share confidences with just yet. Instead she entertained herself by using her skills as a seamstress to make me beautiful clothes, and entertained me with girly pursuits.

It was the early eighties, so I'd dress in flared blue jeans and woolly jumpers that Mum or Gran knitted for me. For some reason they were often burgundy coloured, with knitted pom poms attached to every spare inch. I must have looked like something that had fallen off a Christmas tree. My hair was a dark blonde colour, thick and shiny and so long it went right down to my bum. If I was tired, cold or shy I could even use it as a blanket to hide under.

Every Sunday before chapel, Mum loved to play with my hair. She'd use sponge rollers to make it fall into big, loose curls, then pin each side of hair away from my face with two tortoiseshell clips. People must have thought it was a little china doll taking her place on one of the pews. Mum liked to experiment with different hair styles, from French plaits that were fashionable then, to cute bunches that made the neighbours coo. By washing, brushing and styling my hair, Mum bonded with me, and it was our time together as the women of the house.

I must have come across as a spoilt little brat, what with Grandad popping by with presents every other day too. Everyone made a fuss over me.

Just over a year after I was born Mum had another little boy, my brother Richard, but as the only girl in the house I still got special attention. I'd sit in front of the TV in my brown pinafore dress and white knee-high socks and watch my favourite programmes while Mum brushed my hair which was comforting and cosy for both of us.

My mother had bright red hair, although she always claimed it was blonde. Like mine, it was long and straight and went right down her back. She had sparkling green eyes, like stained glass with the sun shining through, and she was tiny.

I'd sit and watch intently as she put her blue eyeliner on – then I'd try to copy her and make a mess of my face. She was always so glamorous, with pointy nails that were manicured to perfection. If she broke a nail it was as though the world was coming to an end. There'd be wailing round the house as if someone had died. It made

Dad laugh, and that just made her more cross. Mum loved to play music as she got ready for a night out, and she'd tong her hair then set it with tons of hairspray. To this day I can't remember the perfume she wore, just the scent of the Ellnet hairspray that wafted after her.

She was a traditionalist – everything about her was ultra-feminine and our home was so pristine it looked like a show house. When people came round to visit, they would comment that you couldn't believe kids lived there. She really cared about other people's opinions. As well as wanting to create a nice family home, it mattered to her what the neighbours thought.

Mum and Dad were like chalk and cheese. He was tall, with dark brown hair and puppy-brown eyes. Back then he had long hair and wore big shirts with pointy collars that made him look like a mad wizard. He was more relaxed about life too. He loved sixties music, so the stereo would often be rocking to the sounds of the Stones or the Doors, and Dad would be grooving along with his big, happy smile. Sometimes he would pick me up from school on his moped, grinning conspiratorially as he passed me my little helmet. The other kids thought it was really cool, and I'd feel very grown-up and lucky to have such an exciting dad.

These first five years of my life were idyllic. But if life seemed wonderful, it was about to come crashing down around me.

I was too young to realize it but my parents' marriage was falling apart.

The puppy love that had propelled them down the

aisle wasn't enough to help them cope with the realities of married life with three kids.

In a way, the relationship had been doomed from the start.

Mum and Dad were both sixteen when they first met. Mum was a machinist in a sewing factory and Dad was the mechanic who would come round to repair any faults. These were their first jobs since leaving school, and their first faltering footsteps into the world of adulthood. The truth is they were still kids playing around at life but, unfortunately, there were adult consequences to their fun: Mum fell pregnant, long before she was mature enough to cope with it, and back then women didn't have choices – especially when they were from a staunch Catholic family. Breaking the news must have been one of the hardest thing she's ever done. Mum's father had already passed away, or no doubt my own dad wouldn't have lived to see his first child. As it was, Mum was faced with two stark options: get married or be sent away to have the baby and then give it up when it was born. Abortion was out of the question.

Another complicating factor was my dad's religion; he was Protestant. It was probably a close second in shame that not only was my mother with child, but by a Protestant too. When you walked into my maternal gran's house it was like walking into an annexe of the Vatican. Beautiful icons, glazed in gold, gazed down from the walls. There was even a dish of holy water by the door to purify yourself as you entered. Mum always joked it was probably a way of spiritually disinfecting Dad when he came in.

But the fact was, having a baby out of wedlock was unthinkable in those days. Any husband – even one with the wrong God – was better than none, so they decided to get married. They were in love, but chances are it was puppy love, rather than anything more substantial. Dad admits that if Mum hadn't fallen pregnant they wouldn't have got married so young.

With a baby on the way, and disapproving family on the sidelines, there was no fairytale wedding to celebrate their union. Instead, they got married in a register office – Dad in his best trousers and Mum in her best frock. There was no morning suit or wedding dress. Afterwards they went to the cinema. That was as close as they got to a honeymoon. A few months later Tom came into the world to little fanfare.

If people did the maths, they were too polite to say.

They were a family now and had to get on with it.

Now, over five years later, that family was starting to disintegrate.

I heard them rowing, but with Dad at work most of the time it didn't seem to dominate the household. Looking back, he was obviously spending all his time working to avoid being at home with Mum.

Family holidays had always been lots of fun. Mum and Dad singing along to Dire Straits on the radio while my two brothers and me were squeezed together on the back seat of the car, me belting the song out at the top of my tiny lungs. We'd never go anywhere fancy as money was always tight. But when you're a kid, going to a caravan park is just as thrilling as going to Disneyland. Your imagination fills in the blanks that money can't.

I didn't worry about making do, because Grandad bought me all the plush presents my parents couldn't afford, so I never went without. Holidays were about spending time with the family, and that was what really counted for me.

That all changed. Suddenly Mum started taking us to the caravan park on her own. Grandad would drive us down, then pick us up again at the end of the week. We all sat in the car in glum silence wondering why Dad was too busy with work to come with us. It wasn't just his job that he distracted himself with. He'd also become obsessed with CB radio – a walkie talkie device popular back then, in the days before mobile phones. Mum hated how much time he spent with the radios; she felt he didn't give her any attention.

The rows escalated, like the background hum of static interference. When I lay in bed trying to sleep and when I woke up in the morning, I could here them bickering, shouting, throwing accusations at each other. I didn't understand what they meant, but I knew it was bad news. When it all got too much I'd huddle up with Tom. He became like a second dad to me during those turbulent times.

Then my perfect world fell apart for good.

I was six years old, and although I didn't know it then, the fairytale childhood I'd mostly enjoyed so far was about to end abruptly.

'We have to talk.'

Those were the words that greeted us when Dad came home from work that night. I sat on his knee, twirling the ribbons in my hair anxiously.

'Grandad's gone away on a training course, so I'm moving in with Gran to keep her company.'

'Why?' I asked, confused.

'Because Gran will be sad without him.'

'But we'll be sad without you,' I replied, my lower lip trembling.

He looked thrown for a moment, then pulled himself together.

'You've got your mum to look after you, Gran's got no one.'

I looked down at my brown buckled shoes in silence and bit my lip. Dad was leaving us and I felt abandoned. Was it my fault? I wondered. This was to be the story of my life. When the adults messed up, I blamed myself.

But there was one person who I could rely on: Grandad.

Unlike my own house, where rows destroyed any feeling of peace or security, my grandparents' house was an oasis of calm. Gran and Grandad appeared to have a rock-solid marriage. She worshipped him with quiet dedication. She cooked, cleaned, worked and never once moaned about anything. From the snippets of stories I picked up from other members of the family, Grandad had been a Jack the Lad in his teens. But he'd met Gran when he was twenty-one and a year later married her.

If she was in a good mood, Gran would tell me about their romance. She confessed that part of her wedding dress had been made out of old parachute silk, discarded by the air force. Grandad would chortle at this memory, and I'd pick up their wedding photograph, which took pride of place on the shelf in the living room, to examine it. Gran looked beautiful in her patchwork silk dress, and Grandad looked handsome in his black tie.

They looked happy together

Staring at the young faces smiling out at me in the fairytale wedding snap, I could see the imprint of the old couple they would become. I couldn't believe they were the same people. At that point I couldn't grasp how young people could get so old. But soon my feelings of disbelief turned into something far more sinister. Before long, I'd wonder with horror how that smiling, handsome young man, excited about his future with his new wife, could become a monster who abused his own flesh and blood. What happened? I'd wonder.

What flipped the switch?

2. Tainted Love

When Mum and Dad split up, everything changed. Before, I'd been the centre of everyone's world. Suddenly I was banished to the sidelines.

Dad moved back in with his parents, while Mum tried to adjust to life as a poor, single parent. When Christmas came the local priest dropped round presents for us. Every year they provided gifts donated by fellow church-goers for the underprivileged local children. Mum had given her pound notes to the fund before, but now she was on the receiving end of that charity. She was a proud woman, and it can't have been easy for her. She often went without to provide for us.

During the marriage, she'd sought solace from the rows by spending time with her children, especially sharing girly bonding moments with me. That all stopped after the split. She was working flat out making ends meet, so she couldn't spend as much time with us kids. She also needed to get out and meet other people.

My parents were quick to find comfort in the arms of new partners. Within a matter of months both of them had met someone else, and it felt like I was relegated to the bottom of their list. My elder brother coped well enough with this change, but it was a shock for me. I felt lost in life, like I didn't belong anywhere or to anyone. Gone were the girly nights with my mum styling my hair and laughing as I sang into the hairbrush pretending to be a pop star.

Things got worse when Mum fell pregnant with her new partner. It was so soon after the split it can't have been planned, but she was happy to be starting a new life, and sealing the bond with a new addition to the family.

When Lee arrived, her attention was taken up with her new child. My song and dance routines went unnoticed as she dedicated herself to feeding him, soothing his crying and looking after his every whim. What I felt was far deeper than jealousy. Sibling rivalry is always hard to cope with, but fast on the heels of the divorce it was unbearable for me. I felt as though my life had been shattered.

But as if this wasn't bad enough, my life was about to take another turn for the worse.

Shortly after having the baby my mother discovered she had breast cancer. At the time I was too young to understand what was happening. No one explained why she was so sick – I just knew she was poorly and had to spend a lot of time in hospital. Family and neighbours rallied round, looking after us on the days she was having treatment, but we missed her.

Looking back, I understand the hell she must have gone through. Coping with three young kids and a baby, then having to deal with the shock of a cancer diagnosis must have been very traumatic. But I was only six at the time, and all I knew was that my family was like a spinning top whirling out of control. I felt scared for the future, and sorry for myself.

Who would look after me? I worried, watching Mum

go off for hospital appointments. Now I had to become my own mum.

I'd sit in my room brushing my hair, my small fingers fumbling to get it into the plaits Mum loved me to wear. Tears would prick my eyes and I'd bite my lower lip to stop myself from letting the sobs I was holding in flood out.

I had to grow up – and fast. I became self-sufficient, keeping problems to myself, rather than worry my mum with them.

Snuggling under my pink duvet at night I felt alone and unloved.

But someone was about to profit from my misery.

During these difficult times, one person's love and attention for me was constant. When I felt low and abandoned, there was always someone to reassure me that I was still his special little girl.

Grandad had been waiting for this moment, and now he pounced.

With Dad living at his house, suddenly he had intimate access to me – and I was in no emotional state to resist when his sick attacks began.

Before the divorce and Mum's illness, I'd never spent extended periods of time alone with Grandad. I'd visit his house for an afternoon, or he'd take me out with my brothers in tow, but we were never alone for too long. But during the time we did spend together he made a real fuss of me. He'd take us out to the swing park, where my brothers would run off together to play football, and I'd be left alone with Grandad. Usually I was wearing a pinafore dress, and I always had my hair in a high ponytail, just the way he liked it. I hate to admit it now, but those were some of the happiest times of my life. We were so close people would describe us as two peas in a pod. Walking along together, hand in hand, life seemed perfect.

There was a lake nearby, and in the summer Grandad would take me out canoeing. We'd giggle together as the boat rocked from side to side.

'Mind you don't fall out!' he'd yell, grabbing hold of me to make sure I was safe. Sometimes I'd do it on purpose so he could save me.

When I looked up at him with my big, blue eyes they must have been full of adoration. He was my world. With him, I was wrapped in cotton wool.

In the winter, we'd skate in our shoes on the frozen lake. I can remember our screeches of pleasure reverberating round the leafless trees. I'd hold onto Grandad's coat to stop myself falling over. The boys would skate off into the distance at high speed. But I was always by his side, humming happily and chattering nineteen to the dozen with the kind of silly talk young girls love.

I never questioned why he enjoyed these outings so much. Why would I?

He lavished attention and gifts on me, and I assumed all grandads acted like this.

One day during a shopping trip I spotted a toy I desperately wanted. It was every young girl's dream. I'd never seen anything like it before, and my eyes widened with wonder. It was a rag doll – with an expensive price tag. She had blonde pigtails clipped with red bows and a red dress, but if you lifted up her skirt and turned her upside down there was another doll, with long brunette woolly hair and a bright blue polka-dot dress.

I flipped her inside out time and time again, then looked pleadingly at my grandad. His face broke into a wide smile.

'Go on then, have it,' he told me conspiratorially, ruffling my hair.

I jumped up and down with excitement, and gave him a big hug, my little arms only reaching to the top of his legs.

He glanced around to check no one was listening, then bent down and whispered in my ear.

'But it's our secret, don't tell your mum and dad.'

I nodded my head, promising not to tell another soul about it.

I kept the doll at his house, so my parents never knew about my growing stash of expensive toys. When I went round to Grandad's I'd rush upstairs to play with them, singling out the rag doll as my favourite. I never understood why it had to be kept a secret, but I was too happy to care.

And so the grooming began.

Abuse from a family member isn't like an attack from a stranger. There's nothing sudden or random about it. It's premeditated to the nth degree; it requires a careful, cunning strategy to set in place the tools of manipulation for the future. So during those innocent outings in the crisp, fresh air of winter days, and the happiness in secret shopping trips, a seed was planted: me and Grandad had secrets, and I mustn't tell.

But at this point, these were nice secrets I was happy

to keep. They weren't associated with pain and fear. After the divorce, these secrets took on a dark edge. Grandad didn't need to take me out any more: instead I was delivered right to his door.

The arrangement was that Dad would see us kids at weekends. At first, he was still living at Grandad's, so this meant we'd go to his. Because I was Grandad's favourite, I had to stay over on Saturday nights.

In all my young life I'd never slept away from home for the night before. But I was excited to be going to see my dad, and get a chance to play with my toys.

Grandad picked me up in the car. My little legs dangled over the front seat, and my feet didn't quite touch the floor. I jabbered excitedly as we drove along the narrow country roads, racing past the river and finally emerging into the hustle of a small town, overshadowed by grey cloud and misty rain. I'd visited lots of times before, but this time, with an overnight bag packed with my favourite Minnie Mouse nightie, I savoured every detail of this new adventure. Things were difficult at home, so I welcomed a weekend away.

My grandparents' house was situated in a courtyard, with the front door leading onto a concrete square with a huge boulder in the middle, which I fantasized was a spaceship. It was a spooky, sombre place with a cold atmosphere. There were houses on either side, adjacent and opposite. Windows looked in from every angle, as if unblinking eyes were silently watching over you. At the back, patio doors looked out onto a small garden with a low fence. With the houses crowded together, there was no sense of privacy.

As we walked through the front door, Gran looked up from the stove in the kitchen. 'Will you be all right to look after her, love?' she asked Grandad, unfastening her apron and looking anxiously at her watch.

Dad had already gone off to work, so I had to wait until the morning to see him. He'd just joined the police force and had thrown himself into the long hours and that included overtime at the weekends. Gran also worked in the evenings, including Saturdays, at a local hotel. She usually finished about one in the morning and got up in time to make breakfast. The plan was that Grandad would bath me, put me to bed, and then settle in for a quiet night on his own, watching telly, getting some time to himself.

'No problem, it'll be a pleasure to have the wee bairn around,' said Grandad settling into his special chair, smiling as I raced upstairs to get my rag doll.

Everything was immaculately tidy in the house under Gran's watchful eye. So as I spread my toys out over the brown carpet, imprinted with a murky leaf pattern, I looked up to check it was okay to make a bit of a mess. Grandad winked at me indulgently, then picked up his newspaper from the sideboard and started reading the local sports results.

Bored with my toys, I eventually got up and started to do a tap-dance routine, begging Grandad to look at me. He glanced over the top of his newspaper and said, 'Very good,' before going back to his reading.

I stuck a hip out, sighed in mock exasperation, and said, 'No, Grandad, watch *properly*. I'm doing a dance for you – look how good I am.'

At this, he put his paper down and gave me his full attention. I twirled round, bumping my ankle on the side of the grey sofa, then started again.

Gran frowned as she squeezed past me to leave the house, saying, 'Make sure she behaves herself. She needs to be in bed by eight thirty at the latest.' Then looking towards me added, 'Be a good girl for your grandad.'

With a dismissive flick of his hand, he acknowledged what she'd said, and then went back to clapping my performance.

The door clicked shut behind Gran, automatically locking us in.

I carried on singing along to the radio in a high-pitched voice, trying to get the heel-toe-heel combination of my dance right, totally absorbed in what I was doing. My ponytail swished from side to side in time with the music.

'Right, bath time for you, young lady,' he announced suddenly, standing up in a determined fashion. He was over six feet tall, towering above me. I looked questioningly at the clock. It was only six thirty – too early for a bath. If he saw me glance at the time in confusion, he didn't acknowledge it. Instead, he put his large hand on my shoulders and pivoted me round towards the bottom of the stairs.

I shrugged to myself and cantered up the stairs trying to see if I could jump two steps at a time. This was obviously the way it worked at Grandad's house, I thought to myself. It wasn't my usual routine, but lately, nothing seemed to be the way it had been before. I was getting used to change.

The bathroom was small and claustrophobic, with a

small frosted-glass window. The only time there was any natural light was when the top section was ajar. The room had a slightly damp, fusty smell.

It felt odd to be with Grandad in such a small space. I was used to walking through the park, or skating on the lake with him. Open, outdoor places with a canopy of crisp, clean sky overhead seemed natural, but inside felt strange.

This close I could smell the old tobacco on his clothes. As he reached forward to tug my hand-knitted pink cardie off I could see where the yellow tips of his broad fingers had been stained by years of smoking Golden Virginia. I always watched in fascination as his fingers deftly conjured the rolling papers and tobacco into a cigarette, like a magician. But it felt different now these tainted fingers were prying my clothes off. Usually it was only my mum who ever undressed me, not even Dad did that.

The ultra-clean white tiles gave the room a clinical feel, and I felt as though I was preparing for a doctor's examination rather than a bath.

'Pop yourself on the toilet,' he ordered me, a slight flush tinging his cheeks. His fingers fumbled with the brown laces of my shoes as he tried to untie them, eventually tugging them off, then putting them side by side right next to the bathroom door. I looked at them from my vantage point on the toilet with Grandad bent on his knees in front of me, and the thought flickered through my mind that the shoes were waiting to escape, to run out of the room.

My toes curled up involuntarily with cold when I stood

on the floor, as he pulled my brown bobble jumper over my head, messing up my ponytail, so wisps of hair fell round my face, tickling the sides of my cheeks. I still had my white vest on, tucked into my knickers, but I folded my arms across my chest, in an automatic gesture of protection. As he slid my brown cord trousers down, he mumbled under his breath, saying that I was all dirty and 'needed a good clean'.

I lifted my arms above my head so he could take my vest off, not sure if I needed to reply to his mutterings, but feeling more uncomfortable by the minute. All I knew was I didn't feel right about things.

But Grandad was very matter of fact. 'Pop your knickers off and get in the bath,' he told me, trailing his stained fingers through the water to check the temperature. I found this movement reassuring – it was what Mum did.

So as Grandad held my hand I climbed into the bath. I was too innocent to translate my uneasiness into words, and just did as I was told.

Looking back I often ask myself, 'Why was I so spooked?'

I was very young, knew absolutely nothing about sex, had never been ashamed of being naked before, but somehow I just *knew*. All my primal instincts were kicking in and warning, DANGER.

Small memories flashed back into my consciousness. Afternoons out with Grandad when I'd accidentally got my top dirty. Back at home, he'd often tell me, 'Take your top off, it needs a wash,' and would then kiss and cuddle me as I shivered in my vest, willing the tumble dryer to whirl round faster. Dad never did this, and Mum would only purse her lips in annoyance if I got myself in a mess, and order me to go upstairs and change.

It was as if these individual, incidental memories were coming together to form a bigger picture in my mind to warn me. With a pensive look on my face I splashed the water in the bath with none of my usual exuberance.

I wasn't frightened – fear needs something from the past to feed off. It never occurred to me that my grand-father would hurt me sexually – it was beyond my comprehension. I was just as likely to expect a big blue elephant to fly through the window. But I was wary, like an animal on high alert, guarding itself against unknown threats. Kids are very straightforward. If they don't like something, they're very aware of their feelings. I wasn't at all happy.

'I can't believe how dirty you are,' he said again, pick-ing up a loofah from the side of the bath and vigorously scrubbing me with it.

After a few minutes he slackened off, content I was clean. Now he became more playful, leaning over the bath, a lock of Brylcreemed hair falling across his face as he tried to reach me.

'This is a new game,' he told me, tickling my sides so I splashed about in the bath, squirming to get away, giggling frantically.

We'd played the cuddle game before, but his hands were more adventurous now, they weren't confined to a bear hug.

'Get off!' I squealed. It was only a game, but there was a touch of hysteria in my voice. The ceiling seemed to be closing in on me, and I wanted to be tucked up in bed, with my rag doll sleeping safely by my side.

'Look over there,' he said, nodding towards the taps. A showerhead was attached to the top of them, and a metal overflow was beneath them.

'Spiders crawl out of the hole, you know?' He told me with a knowing grin on his face. I looked wide-eyed towards the overflow, picturing horrible black legs poking out and coming to get me. I was terrified of spiders. Before I could recoil, Grandad started tickling my feet.

'The spiders crawl up your legs, and scuttle around you.' He laughed, running his fingertips up the inside of my legs, then moving up to tickle my sides, brushing between my legs as he did. I giggled nervously, trying to push him off me. The game lasted for about fifteen minutes, his fingers fleetingly touching me in private places. It was all so fast, the movements were just glancing, passing flicks and strokes, that didn't linger long enough for me to get seriously scared. But I felt very disturbed by the game, for reasons I was too young to quite understand.

To this day, I have to hide the overflow with a flannel when I have a bath. An unknown fear has been hard-wired into my brain.

Afterwards, he dried me with a bright blue towel, telling me what a good girl I'd been. 'You're my special girl.' He winked, rubbing the towel all over my body. He then pulled my pink and white Minnie Mouse nightie over my head, which had the word 'sleepy' on the front and 'time' on the back.

'Now run along to bed,' he told me, walking downstairs to roll a cigarette.

I climbed into bed with my little heart pounding. My chest felt tight and my breathing was shallow and rapid. I never usually felt like this after my bath, and I knew that something was seriously wrong, but I couldn't say why. In the same way I had sensed there was more to the story than met the eye when Dad had walked out of our family home with just an overnight bag under the pretence he was looking after Gran. Dad had never returned home, and our idyllic life had been shattered, our family broken apart. What horrible changes in my life did this new development signal?

I searched my mind, trying to figure out why the grandad I loved so much had made me feel so bad. It didn't make any sense. I grabbed my rag doll, turning her inside out to the brunette with the blue polka-dot dress. She was the one who I turned to when I was upset. I whispered in her ear, asking her if all grandads bathed their special little girls in that way. I cuddled her tight for comfort, and tried to pull my nightie down below my knees. I wanted to be covered and wrapped up safe.

After a few moments my eyes adjusted to the dark, and I could see the starlit night through the gap between the curtains. I stared towards them in a daze. In the dusky light the unicorn-patterned wallpaper seemed to come alive. I could almost imagine the magical, mythical beasts jumping down off their safe perch on the wall to help me, cantering round the room, consoling me. Grandad had told me they only appeared to good virtuous girls, and that their fantastical single horn on the top of their head was used to banish evil people. I prayed that the fleet of silvery, grey unicorns would come to my rescue. But I still wasn't sure who I needed saving from.

The three-piece wardrobe loomed ominously, like a dark shadow over my bed. I imagined this was a big giant coming to get me, and shrank down underneath my covers, clutching my rag doll even tighter.

Suddenly I heard the creak of floorboards outside my door. The landing light was switched on and a ray of light flooded under the gap between my door and the carpet. Grandad was coming to kiss me night night.

The door opened slowly, and his shadow loomed over the bed, bigger even than the wardrobe I'd been scared of earlier.

'Are you asleep yet?' he asked in a quiet voice, walking towards the bed

I shook my head. For now, I had no real reason to lie to him.

'Shall I tuck you in?'

I nodded my head, poking my arms out over the covers, and resting my rag doll on the pillow next to my head, so she could be tucked in too.

He strode in and the stench of rolling tobacco trailed behind him.

The spare room I slept in contained a single bed, made up just as Gran always liked it, in case they had guests stay over. She always used starched, old-fashioned linen and thought duvets were the work of the devil. She was a very precise woman, and the linen sheets were stretched taut, so it became like a straightjacket when you got inside. On top was a brown, itchy blanket that looked like it belonged in an old Victorian hospital.

Grandad bent over the bed and tugged at the sheets, making sure they were all arranged nicely, so none of the cold air would waft in and chill me. He switched the lamp on and sat on the edge of the bed. The wardrobe went back to its usual shape, and the unicorns stared listlessly from the walls, returning to their two-dimensional positions.

'It's going to be fun now you can spend more time here with me, isn't it?'

I agreed weakly, torn between genuinely agreeing, and still feeling weird about what had happened when he gave me a bath.

Then Grandad starting talking to me in a calm, reassuring voice.

Looking back, I now see that the words dripping out his mouth were the most evil, manipulative sentences anyone could ever say to a little girl. But then, I lay in bed, the sheets hemming me in, listening with horror to what he had to say but at the same time feeling hugely grateful that at least I had one person who still loved me, even if he did give me strange baths.

'You know how much I love you, don't you?' he asked.

I smiled back, showing one tooth missing that the tooth fairy had taken.

'It's such a shame that Mummy and Daddy don't love you any more ...' He trailed off and looked out of the window thoughtfully.

My stomach tensed with anxiety. I knew my parents were too busy to spend much time with me at the moment, but it had never occurred to me that they'd stopped loving me. But what he was saying *did* make sense. It explained why Daddy didn't want to live with us any more, and why Mummy didn't have time to brush my hair now. Tears of rejection stung my eyes. Mummy and Daddy had stopped loving me.

'But I'll always love you.' He looked down at me, and stroked the hair from my forehead, smiling gently. 'Even if your mum and dad decide to send you away, I'll never let that happen, you can come here and live with me.'

A look of fear spread across my face. 'They'd send me away? Why? Where to?' I tried to pull myself up on the pillow and sit up. This news had shocked me to the core.

Grandad looked serious and full of concern.

'Well, they might not want you any more. They're not interested in you, and they might want to give you away to an orphanage.'

A stray tear rolled down my face.

Grandad, wiped it away. 'Don't worry, you'll always have me.'

As he walked out, switching the light off after him, a bigger fear loomed in my mind – bigger than anything I'd ever dreamt of before. Parents could actually give their little girls away.

Suddenly bath time wasn't the biggest worry on my mind; it was a price I'd have to pay if I wanted Grandad to keep loving me. Otherwise *no one* would want me.

For a young child, that is the worst fear of all.

3. Special Games

'Grandad's here,' Mum shouted up the stairs to me. I walked slowly down, counting the steps as I went – twenty, same as always. There weren't enough as far as I was concerned. I wished there were thousands and I could spend years walking down those stairs never arriving at the bottom.

It was Saturday. Again. It seemed to come round quicker and quicker as every week went by. I couldn't believe it was only a month ago I'd skipped into the car, excited about the adventure of staying over for the first time.

After that first bath time I'd wondered why I'd felt so uneasy.

Now I knew why.

I could hear Mum and Grandad making polite conversation. He was asking after baby Lee, and Mum was commenting on a bad accident, which all the locals were still gossiping about. Grandad kept a professional silence, not slipping in any details that would have kept the grapevine busy. He could be very taciturn when it suited him. Standing there with Mum, he looked the picture of a responsible adult, respected paramedic and loving grandfather.

For a while their conversation turned to Mum's health,

and I could hear by the tone of her voice she was paying close attention to his opinions. He was a trained medic, after all. She was on the mend, and the cancer seemed to be responding to the treatment. I couldn't quite grasp what that meant, but the atmosphere of panic in the house had calmed down slightly.

But that didn't ease my worries. Now Grandad had planted the seed in my mind I had to be vigilant every second in case she planned to give me away. I ran to check the post first, as if it was a new game I liked to play. Secretly, I was checking the postmarks to see if any letters were from potential children's homes. When the phone rang, I was first to answer it, often panting and out of breath, grabbing the receiver if my brothers got there before me. I had to monitor who was calling the house. I lived every day at home as if it might be my last. The more peculiar my behaviour got, the more I annoyed my mother, and the more she fussed over my brothers instead.

I would interpret little things she said as proof she didn't love me any more. When she told me off for making up silly stories I'd run up to my room and sob into my pillow wondering what I'd done to deserve this. If I heard her muttering to her new partner in the bedroom, I'd sneak up and try to overhear what they were saying. Standing rigid I'd try and decipher every muffled word to see if they were discussing me and what to do about me. Sometimes Mum would genuinely be having a moan about me and my odd behaviour, and my knees would almost buckle beneath me. Everything Grandad says is true, I'd think to myself.

My heart would sink and I'd trudge back to my bedroom, despondent.

If Mum didn't love me any more that meant Grandad was the only person in my life I could count on. Just like he said, he was all I had.

But over the last few weeks this had become an increasingly terrifying prospect. For years all I'd had to do to earn the accolade of 'good girl' was sing his favourite songs, play nicely and generally just be myself.

Now the stakes had been raised much higher.

I wasn't his good girl any more because I *wanted* to be, but because I was frightened *not* to be. What I had to do to deserve his love was changing.

I didn't understand it, but I hated it.

Bath time had become a code word for entering a private world with Grandad, which was unlike anything I'd ever experienced in my life before. It was like slipping into a bad movie I couldn't escape from. Afterwards, I was always left with the uneasy feeling a nightmare brings on, which casts a dark shadow over every part of your day. It felt like a slimy gloom was swallowing me up, tainting every part of my life.

Now, walking down the stairs to meet my grandad, the feeling of doom intensified.

'Here she is, my beautiful little girl.' He beamed as I came to the bottom of the stairs, hiding slightly behind my mum's legs.

'Say hello to your grandad,' said Mum impatiently, as I skulked in the background. 'Kids, eh?' She smiled, handing him my overnight bag.

I gave him a weak smile and went over to say hello. My

hair was loose, flowing down my back. It was a little point of rebellion, not to wear it the way he liked it, because in every other way, I had to do what he said.

We drove over to his house in silence, the radio playing chart hits and the DJ talking inanely over the top as the songs played out. I couldn't help but tap along with my feet. Music was one of the only joys in my life.

In a strange way I was glad to be with him, pleased that he still cared enough to come and pick me up, keen to look after me and show interest in my life. I was relieved he still loved me, but scared of the price I had to pay for it.

When we arrived, Dad was still at home. I ran up and threw my arms round him. I missed not having him about. He seemed genuinely pleased to see me and planted a kiss on my forehead. I started talking nineteen to the dozen about my week at school, telling him about a school show I was in. It was going to be a big deal, and all the other kids' parents were going. My dream was that my mum and dad would patch things up for the night and both come to see me. I figured they'd be so proud of me they'd realize they really did love me after all, and that I was good enough to be their daughter.

'You will come, Daddy, won't you?' I asked pleadingly.

'We'll see,' he said in a preoccupied tone. 'I might have to work that night, but I'll do my best.' With that he ruffled my hair, and headed upstairs to get ready for his evening shift. He would be working, I was sure.

I felt totally deflated. From the corner of my eye I could see Grandad smiling knowingly. I knew what he was thinking – 'told you so'.

My weekends at my grandparents' had settled into a steady routine, and I could see Gran pottering about in the kitchen making dinner for Grandad to eat after she'd left. She'd make me a cheese sandwich, so he didn't have to bother doing anything but giving me my bath. As far as she was concerned, this was the only inconvenience he had to put up with in this new arrangement. She had no idea how keen he was to get me naked, and alone.

Dad bounded down the stairs in his police uniform. His black trousers had been perfectly pressed by my gran, and his hat sat proudly on his head.

I saw policemen patrolling the streets, and Mum always told me to let them know if any strange men tried talking to me. 'A policeman will make sure you're safe,' she had said, making me promise to always ask for help.

But even though my own father was a policeman, he had no idea about the danger I was facing. I couldn't keep my promise to my mum, because it wasn't a stranger who was hurting me, it was my own grandad. She never included family members in her warnings, and that confused me.

I watched forlornly as Gran left for work, munching on my cheese sandwich without much appetite. Rag doll was on the floor beside me, her blonde bunches highlighted by the murky brown of the carpet.

'Bath time.' Grandad smirked, stubbing his cigarette out.

Since that first time, things had got so much worse.

I climbed the stairs, dragging my feet as he led the way, his big boots clunking with every step he took. A waft of his Old Spice aftershave followed behind him, a scent that clogged up my throat with fear.

'I bet you're all dirty again,' he said, pulling off my clothes, tutting to himself. Even though I was terrified of what was about to happen, I was still too young to know what it was or to realize how wrong it was.

Maybe I *was* very dirty, I thought to myself. Nobody loved me any more, so it made sense that other things about me were bad too. All this went round my mind as I searched for answers I was too young to find, for questions I wasn't even sure I should be asking. But as soon as I stood there naked, shivering in the cold air, I was overwhelmed by misery.

'Look what I've bought you,' said Grandad leering over me as I tried to sink my body as far as I could into the lukewarm water.

He was holding a posh-looking bar of soap in his hand, wrapped up in expensive white paper. 'It's a special soap to get you clean,' he told me, unwrapping it and dunking it in the water. A sickly musky perfume drifted towards me, a smell I somehow associated with grown-ups.

He started soaping me down, making sure not to miss a single inch of my body. I tensed against his touch, trying to pull away. The first time he'd been very gentle with me, and his touches had been very subtle. But with each week that went by, he gradually dropped the pretence of not interfering with me, and his touches became more deliberate and less disguised as accidental.

When he could feel me pull away from him Grandad became cross, and his cajoling tone took on a nasty edge. 'Don't be a bad girl,' he admonished me, his hands becoming rougher with impatience. 'You need to be clean.'

I sat there silently, and before I could stop them, tears started to stream down my face. I tried to brush them away, but he noticed them tracking down my face. 'Why are you crying?' he said brusquely, yanking me round so he could wash my back. His mouth was pursed with annoyance. 'You're getting to be a big girl now, and we need to clean your special place.' He stopped as he said this, looking directly at me. 'Stand up,' he ordered, reaching out to hold my hand.

I tentatively put my hand in his to stop myself slipping over as I attempted to pull myself upright. The smell of his aftershave and the cloying smell of the soap mixed together. Tears spilled down my face.

'Stand with your legs apart,' he commanded, prising them open with his nicotine-stained hand, which felt cold and rough on my skin.

I did as I was told, feeling more exposed and afraid than ever.

'Now you're becoming a big girl you need to smell clean down there,' he told me as he started to rub the soap roughly over my private parts.

I started sobbing, the kind of tears that jam in your throat, making you speechless, stinging your eyes with pressure. Finally, when a sob racked my body, my chest would shudder in spasms, and a sound, like that of an injured woodland animal, would come out, as if it didn't belong to me.

It's hard to put into words what I was feeling. At such a young age it is best expressed through the language of dreams – nightmare worlds and monsters. Like all young children, I was very sensitive, emotionally and physically, so these starting steps in the abuse were torture for me. Especially because at this point I hadn't developed any defence mechanism to cope with what was happening. At the beginning, I couldn't disguise my raw emotional distress.

For half an hour I stood in the freezing cold, with cramp gripping my legs as they tensed against this invasion. His face changed, as if a dark cloud had passed over it. It was like he was possessed. I was in incredible pain, his touch was hard and forceful, but more than anything it was my heart that was breaking. I loved Grandad, and I couldn't understand why he needed to hurt me like this. Mum had never done this to me, neither had Dad.

My tears welled into great big sobs that shook my tiny little frame.

I didn't want him to do this to me, but I also knew I couldn't tell.

It was our little secret. He hadn't spelt it out yet, but he had dropped hints about what would happen to me if I confessed to anyone. I would be sent away for ever, with no one to love me or care about me. I also knew that if I mentioned what he'd done to anyone, they probably wouldn't believe me. He'd just dismiss it, saying, 'Och, I was just washing her, she's talking nonsense.' Back then child abuse wasn't talked about, so people weren't overly suspicious about this kind of behaviour.

Also, I'd been playing up since the divorce – I liked to show off and tell fantastical stories to get people's attention. So I knew the grown-ups thought I was prone to silliness and making things up. Now I was scared they would write off any accusations as me being over-imaginative.

I'd lost count of the times I'd heard my family say, 'Its just Emily being Emily,' in a slightly dismissive tone. I was a bundle of energy, who liked to sing and dance and play around, who wanted love more than anything in the world. After the divorce, I was frightened my parents might stop loving me. The more I was ignored the more needy I became, and the more I did all those annoying little things kids do when they're trying to make adults notice them – anything I thought would get a laugh. I'd go over the top, repeating what I'd said, louder and louder, looking for approval. Other times, I'd be sulky and uncommunicative, convinced that no one wanted me and it wasn't even worth trying to make them like me again. I'd sit in a corner and sullenly play with my toys. If someone tried to give me a hug, I'd shrug them off and go upstairs to be alone. I swung from one extreme mood to another, hitting every feeling in between, in an off-kilter rollercoaster of emotions.

Grandad's games had put this behaviour into over-drive. But everyone still put it down to the divorce. No one suspected any other reason.

For my parents, both going through difficult changes in their own lives, it must have been exhausting. But they didn't know the poison I was being fed to stir up my insecurities. So to them I became a problem child it was difficult to get through to. Telling them that Grandad, the only person who seemed to love me and like having me around, was hurting me would have been emotional suicide. As far as they were concerned, I was the problem and Grandad was the solution. So I was his, completely.

After Grandad had finished his 'special wash' the tears just kept flowing. I was overwhelmed by fear, pain and, worst of all, betrayal.

'Stopping crying, and be a big girl,' he chastised me again, rubbing me roughly with the towel. As he tried to rub down there I winced in pain. 'Don't be silly,' he said firmly, holding my arm so I couldn't wriggle free.

I kept crying, I couldn't help myself, although my tears had reduced from the heartfelt sobs during the wash into a pitiful whimper.

'It hurts,' I mumbled quietly, afraid of making him angry.

'It's only sore because you didn't keep it clean,' he replied, confusing me with his logic that somehow I'd done something wrong and deserved it.

'I'm a doctor and it's my job to make you better,' he continued, sliding my pyjamas over my head. 'I'm doing it for your sake.'

He guided me out of the bathroom and into my bedroom, the single bed looking cramped and uninviting in the corner. I slid under the sheets, ready to be tucked in like a prisoner. Rag doll was there waiting for me, and I clutched her to me with relief, more tears flowing down my face, as I drew comfort from the company of a stuffed doll. She's my friend, I thought to myself, snuggling up to her. I didn't have anyone to turn to, and rag doll was the one thing that made me feel better.

'I'll just go and make your supper,' said Grandad in

a normal tone of voice, as if nothing untoward had happened. Afterwards, he could click straight back into the way he had always been with me – loving and considerate.

It confused me even more. It was as if I had two grandads, one who I loved to pieces, and one who terrified the life out of me. I knew no one else saw his dark alter ego, but I worried that this demon side would appear more often, so that every time I visited something even worse would happen to me.

I could hear him humming contentedly downstairs in the kitchen as he prepared my food. My stomach was in knots and I felt sick, so the last thing I wanted to do was eat.

After five minutes I heard his heavy footsteps on the stairs and he appeared at the door, with a huge smile on his face. He placed a glass of warm milk on the bedside table and handed me a plate of buttered cream crackers. They stuck in my throat as I tried to swallow them, but I carried on chewing, not wanting to annoy him. He sat and watched me eat, as if all he cared about was my welfare.

'Shall I read you a bedtime story?' he asked, looking sideways so he didn't have to stare straight into my tear-stained face, with my swollen red-rimmed eyes. He loved to tell me fairytales and folklore about the local area, which, according to legend, had been populated by giants, witches, fairies, imps and goblins in times gone by. I loved to hear these stories. Growing up in Scotland, and watching thick mists come across the hills, settling over the river, casting an eerie light on the dense surrounding woodlands, it was easy to imagine a world where magic existed.

Our area had been famous for its covens of witches, and an eighteen-year-old local woman had famously confessed to practising witchcraft in the area in 1662, claiming she could transform herself into a cat, and lure the ships sailing down the river onto the rocks. I was transfixed by stories like this, imagining women with such great powers that they could change the course of a huge ship, and change themselves into other creatures.

Sometimes we'd talk about out folklore round at Great-granny Hobbs', when I visited with Grandad and, as the light faded, she'd regale us with the legends she'd heard when she was a little girl. She was a no-nonsense kind of woman, so to hear these tales from her mouth was like giving them a stamp of truth. Like all fairytales, these stories scared and thrilled me in equal measure. I was desperate to hear them, and had a pleasurable chill running down my spine afterwards. I'd look into the night sky frightening myself with the thought that it was the very same sky the witches had looked into. When Grandad glanced at the clock, as if to say it was time to go, I'd beg her to carry on. He never interrupted her, so if she was in the mood for talking she'd finish the story. If she was tired, she'd promise to finish it off next time we came round, and I'd moan in protest. It wasn't often she was in the mood to indulge me in this kind of talk, so I knew I could wait for months before I heard how it ended. I'd run it through in my mind, over and over, inventing my own ending, which would get more fantastic at every turn.

But tonight, I wasn't interested in magic. I didn't want to hear fanciful stories. I just wanted the pain to go away, and for someone to give me a proper hug, the kind with no agenda, that makes everything feel better. So I shook my head with a tired, defeated attitude. The last thing I wanted was for Grandad to tell me a story. I just wanted to be alone. He shrugged his shoulders and left the room, turning the light off and leaving me in darkness.

I stifled the sound of my tears into rag doll as I cried myself to sleep.

The next day I wondered if he'd mention anything about what had happened. This had gone beyond any touching he'd done before, and I was sure he'd want to explain himself in the morning. I'd woken up early needing the loo. It was like burning daggers when I went, and I tensed in fear wondering what was wrong with me, worried I'd been seriously injured or, worse, that I was actually dying. It was like peeing fire. This was the start of my love affair, minus the love, with urinary infections. My little body, too young to deal with such physical interference, was already rebelling.

I could smell fried eggs downstairs, and my stomach turned. 'Breakfast's ready,' Gran yelled. Then I heard her mutter to Grandad to go and fetch me. So I bolted out of bed and raced down the stairs, stubbing my toe on the skirting board, and dangling rag doll by her hair as I ran.

'Morning, love,' she said, scooping a greasy egg onto a plate, then adding two slices of cold toast on the side. I sat in the kitchen and looked round, more confused than ever. It was the same as usual. Gran was cooking, humming happily to herself as Grandad read the paper and munched on his buttery toast, slurping tea from his chipped white mug.

The mist from the previous day had cleared, and the sun was shining in through the window. 'Nice day,' Gran observed, looking up to the sky.

The pain after my wee was intensifying and I was finding it hard to sit still on the chair. As I wriggled from side to side trying to adjust my pink pyjamas, Gran caught sight of what I was doing and frowned at me.

'Be a lady!' she exclaimed, outraged by my fumblings to try and relieve the pain. Grandad didn't look up from his paper, pretending he hadn't seen.

I blushed and mumbled an apology, feeling dirtier than ever.

Suddenly Grandad looked up from the paper.

'Ask if she's been a good girl or a bad girl,' he said to Gran.

It was a game to him, and I instantly went into a panic.

'So, have you been a good girl?' Gran asked, wiping the dishes.

I looked towards my grandad, gripped with fear. I didn't know what to say. Had I been bad? What we'd done last night had felt bad. Maybe *he* was going to tell on me for being so dirty he'd had to clean me up. I knew how much Gran hated dirt. Cleanliness was next to godliness, she always said.

My eyes met his, mine etched with confusion – and he winked back.

I'd got my answer.

'Yes, she has been a good girl,' he replied on my behalf.

I nodded in silent agreement, looking morosely at my plate.

Like the witches in the stories I loved so much, I had lost track of what made a person good or bad; things were never as they seemed.

The next day I decided to test the water with Mum, to see her reaction.

'I don't like the games Grandad makes me play,' I told her, looking down at the floor nervously. I didn't have the words to describe what he was doing to me, so I could only explain it in the terms he used – as 'games'.

Mum didn't even break off from wiping the table, laughing as she replied, 'Is he making you play dominoes?' I didn't answer, not knowing what to say. 'Old people can be boring,' she continued, 'but your grandad loves you and you must be a good girl for him.'

That phrase again: good girl. Maybe he was right, and all grandads played these games, and I just had to get used to it. Mum hadn't appeared concerned by what I'd said. She certainly hadn't reacted as if he was doing anything wrong. I felt more confused than ever.

The next week she joked to Grandad about our 'games'. I'd never seen the colour drain from his face so fast. When she mentioned dominoes he relaxed a bit, and they'd laughed together about it. I took this as another sign they were somehow in cahoots, and that Mum knew what was going on and either didn't mind or didn't care. I'd never seen Grandad so angry when we were finally alone together. His entreaties shifted to threats, and I was quite clear on what would happen if I ever mentioned it to anyone again.

No one wants you, he hissed vehemently, time and time again.

4. My Good Girl

'Calm down!' My mum shouted at me from the kitchen, but I could see a smile spreading across her face.

I was almost seven, and even though the abuse had been going on for nearly a year, I could still be happy and playful at home.

I ran round the table, twirled round and sang, 'Da da da da da da da ... WONDER WOMAN,' at the top of my lungs.

By this time my brothers were laughing too, shaking their heads comically as if I were nuts. Encouraged by the attention I carried on singing.

> 'Wonder Woman, Wonder Woman.
> In your satin tights,
> Fighting for your rights
> WONDER WOMAN!'

I raced through the living room, wearing a red and white checked tea towel as a makeshift cape, which wafted behind me with a faint smell of gravy stains. On my head was one of mum's gold necklaces that I'd fashioned into a tiara like the one Lynda Carter wore on the show. It kept slipping over my eyes, temporarily slowing down my superhero gallivanting round the house.

I carried on breathlessly singing and running.

'Make a liar tell the truth.
Wonder Woman,
All our hopes are pinned upon you.
And the magic that you do ...'

I stopped suddenly as the front door opened, just managing to avoid slamming straight into my grandad, who had come round to pick me up.

'Sorry, but Emily's not here today,' laughed my mum to Grandad, as he grabbed me by the waist, swinging me round, 'it's Wonder Woman.'

'Who's she when she's at home then?' he asked, winking to my brothers, who were lounging on the sofa, rolling their eyes at my antics.

'I'm an Amazonian woman sent to save the world,' I announced to everybody in the room with a serious expression, enjoying playing to an audience – although by this time, only Grandad was really listening.

'I'm 2,547 years old and I have special powers.'

'Nearly the same age as Grandad then,' quipped one of my brothers, who got a cuff round the ear. Grandad never tolerated any sign of disrespect.

I'd stolen one of Mum's gold belts from her wardrobe, and it was hanging limply from my hips, far too big for me.

'Her power's in her magic belt apparently; if she takes it off she's just an everyday person again,' said Mum, walking into the living room to say a proper hello to Grandad. As she untied her apron, a weary expression crossed her face. 'I'm glad you've got the energy for an Amazonian superhuman being,' she said. 'I certainly haven't.'

It was meant as a joke, but as soon as I heard her comment my face fell.

Grandad was right, Mum had just made it clear she didn't want me.

I took my belt off slowly, and slipped the gold tiara off my head. Back to being Emily, I felt small and powerless all over again. It was one thing to make believe I had magic powers and could spin myself out of any situation, but the truth was I couldn't ... I was stuck in the misery of my life. Witches, Wonder Woman, whatever I wished, I didn't have the ability to escape, or fight the evil villain out to get me. Worse than that, everyone else thought the baddie was a hero sent to save me.

As the car pulled into the road, my heart sank. There were no children playing outside in the courtyard and the silence felt creepy rather than peaceful. Gran had already gone out; she'd had some shopping to do before her evening shift. The door creaked as we walked through into the house, which was chillier than usual, and without Gran in the kitchen, less comforting then ever. 'Come on, Wonder Woman, use your magic powers to get up them stairs,' said Grandad, bundling me along in a rough manner. The sense of excitement in his voice was obvious; he was acting like a greedy child who couldn't wait to unwrap his favourite toy. There was no pretence of normality. No illusion that I needed my tea, or that I could watch telly like a normal kid, or that baths were just a routine necessity before bed. My bath time was a playground for Grandad, and a torture for me.

He tore at my clothes until I was naked, and my belly

let out a small growl of hunger. I'd have to wait until after the ordeal to eat, I thought to myself. My welfare had gone out of the window; all Grandad cared about now were the sick lusts that appeared to be consuming him more and more.

Usually at bath time, Grandad was fully dressed, while I sat naked. But this time, before I got in the bath, Grandad went to his bedroom to get changed. He came back with a self-satisfied grin on his face, wearing a ludicrously short, white towelling dressing gown. I'd never seen him wear it round the house before and, looking back, I'm certain he'd bought it for this purpose.

Sitting on the edge of the bath, like he usually did, something was horribly different. He was naked underneath his robe, and due to its shortness his private parts were exposed, hanging over the side in full view. I said nothing and tried not to look. But with him being so close, and the bathroom being so small, it was impossible not to pass a glance at it, no matter how much I tried not to look in that direction.

When I did, Grandad seized on the moment, as if I'd been ogling him.

'Eh, are you curious?'

Shaking my head with a furious no, I looked down into the murky water at the outline of my spindly pink legs partly obscured by soapy suds.

'I've caught you looking.' He grinned. 'Don't be ashamed, it's only natural now you're a big girl to want to find out more.'

I'd never seen the grown man's parts before, and I

didn't really know what they were. Dad never walked round naked, and my brothers were still only kids themselves, so the sight of Grandad's penis horrified me beyond belief.

'Why don't you touch it?' he asked, barely able to suppress the excitement in his voice. Again, I shook my head and squirmed away.

Touch it,' he repeated, and this time it was a command. The tone in his voice was now steel-edged. He took my hand, which was tiny and limp compared to his big bear grip and guided my hand towards his penis.

As I touched it, he pressed his hand over mine tightly so I couldn't move it away. 'There, I bet you like that don't you?' he said smugly.

My head was spinning. This was all wrong.

With my hand firmly locked in place, his hand started guiding my movements. I knew he was a grown man but I didn't have the terminology to understand what was happening. Looking back with an adult perspective, I now understand that he became hard. But as a young child I was terrified, wondering what was happening under my hand. Even though what he was doing was disgustingly abnormal, he got excited and started to show his arousal just like normal people do when they're turned on. His breathing came in scary rasps, his body changed, becoming tense, and even his mannerisms were different, more uncontrolled than normal. To a young child, these changes were absolutely terrifying. It got to the point where I understood that what I was doing was creating some kind of physical change in my grandad, but I had no idea why. It scared me to see him behave in this way, but it was more complicated than pure unadulterated fear.

As he kept moving my hand, faster and faster, he started mumbling, saying what a clever girl I was and how happy I was making him.

'This is what all good girls do,' he panted as I glanced at him, terrified by the contorted look on his face. My hand was in agony, aching and crushed by his hand on top; his grip was getting tighter and tighter.

'You're doing such a good job,' he encouraged me when he sensed my arm was about to give way under the pressure.

Suddenly it was over. He dropped my hand, so it splashed in the water. I didn't realize at the time, but he'd climaxed. As far as I was concerned, he was back to normal, and my ordeal was over. I was distraught, but I'd never seen him so pleased with me.

I hated what had just happened, but I also knew that it had made him incredibly happy. He kept telling me how much he loved me and how special I was. Because I believed 110 per cent that if I didn't please him, I would be sent away, I was confused by my own feelings. If I didn't keep him happy then no one would want me.

So where did that leave me? If I told anybody what was happening and made him stop, he wouldn't love me any more. This was the only way I could keep a tenuous hold on the only bit of love I had in my life, even if it disgusted me. I couldn't win, whichever way I looked at things.

Afterwards, I went downstairs to have a late supper. We sat in front of the telly together, Grandad rolling a cigarette as I ate some crackers and cheese.

As he lit up, he gave me a piercing stare and said, 'This is our little secret.'

A threat hung in the air, but it wasn't overt. It wasn't like he'd said, 'If you don't do these things I'm going to stab you.' That's a threat. This was entirely different, but for a child equally as menacing.

'You've been good today,' he continued, puffing slowly so smoke encircled his face, creating a pungent halo. 'But if you're not a good girl next time, then I'll have to tell your mum and dad you've been bad.'

I sniffed, trying not to cry. 'I won't tell,' I promised.

'Good, because your mum doesn't like to show it, but she's told me she loves the new baby much more than you. She really wants to send you away. Don't give her an excuse.'

His words were like a blow to me. I wiped a tear away, and nodded my head.

'You shouldn't spoil her like this,' said Dad, smiling indulgently and putting his arm round Grandad's shoulder with an affectionate squeeze.

'Och, who else can I spend my money on?' Grandad shrugged, trying to play down the shiny wrapped present sitting on the dining table.

It was my seventh birthday, and the smell of home-made sponge cake drifted in from the kitchen. Gran had iced it beautifully, and put on lots of candy-pink candles for me to blow out. Mum hadn't had the time to bake me a cake this year, so I was glad my gran had made one instead.

Dad had even taken a few hours off work so we could celebrate.

'We Are the Champions' by Queen came on the radio and Dad turned it up so it was blasting out. He grinned at me, and we both raised our hands in the air and swung them from side to side, singing along with the anthem. He might have been a policeman, but he could still have some fun when he was in the mood. Sadly, it wasn't that often any more. I missed the carefree, easygoing dad I'd known when I was younger. I didn't understand how stressful working as a new recruit in the police must have been, but I knew that for most of the time, his lips were pursed and his face contracted in a stressful frown as he dashed out of the house to go on duty. There was a lot of responsibility on his shoulders. He took it very seriously, and it took a toll on him.

Grandad was more jovial, even though he had an important job too. He'd been a paramedic for so many years he had become hardened to it. Also, Dad was trying to find his place on the force and prove himself. It was a very macho environment at that time, so he needed to be constantly on the ball and show how committed he was. But Grandad had already proved himself, and he was the kingpin. Sometimes he took me down to the ambulance station with him. All his colleagues would make a fuss of me, and tell me how pretty I was. Grandad would dress me up like a doll he wanted to show off. My hair would be curled and tied up how he liked it, and I'd be wearing my best pinafore dress, with white lace-trimmed ankle socks. I could tell by the deferential way that everyone treated him that he was well respected. 'Want to look in an ambulance?' he'd always say. Inside he'd shut the door behind him, creating a vacuum of silence inside. I could hear the busy chatter outside, like a faraway hum. The smell repulsed me. It was antiseptic mixed with something slightly rancid. He'd show me the machines and tell me about how the wires pumped drugs into people making them fall asleep.

I didn't register it at the time, because I was so compliant, thanks to his manipulations, that anything he wanted to do to me, he could. But when I got older, and the abuse got much worse, having the ability to sedate a person would prove very handy for Grandad. But for now, it just showed me another scary glimpse into the world of grown-ups: a world that disturbed me more with each day that went by.

I knew that people called for ambulances when they'd been hurt and they wanted someone to help them. I tried to work it out in my mind. Grandad hurt me terribly, and I wasn't allowed to tell anyone or ask for help. But when *other* people got hurt, they called for Grandad to come and save them. It just didn't make any sense to me. From a child's view, the world was mad.

Seeing this double life Grandad lived, I slipped into a split personality of my own. It was as if a red hot knife had cut me down the middle. I learned to wear a different mask for every different person I was forced to be.

Today, it was my birthday, so I slipped on my 'loving granddaughter' mask, ready to play the part of the happy-go-lucky child everyone expected me to be, which, more than anything, I longed to be.

My present was wrapped in shiny pink paper, which crinkled up at the sides where it had been sellotaped down.

'Can I open it now?' I asked, jumping up and down on the spot.

'Go on then,' said Grandad, handing it over to me.

I turned it round in my hands a few times first to make the most of the moment. The paper felt smooth and crisp to the touch. Inside felt soft, and I tried to guess what it was, shouting out possibilities, until Gran lost patience with me and told me to get on with it.

Suddenly I started ripping at the paper, like a girl possessed. I was so excited my little hands were shaking as I fumbled to undo the sides and open it up.

First I saw a hint of royal blue, then a flash of cheap, bold yellow-gold, then finally a streak of bright scarlet. I couldn't believe it. I looked up towards Grandad. At moments like this, it was difficult to imagine he was the same man who hurt me. 'Is it really ...?' I trailed off, pulling the costume out with a flourish and smiling so widely it felt as though my face would split.

'WONDER WOMAN!' said Grandad comically, with a triumphant look on his face. 'So do you like it?' he asked.

I was speechless, and Dad answered for me. 'She loves it, but you shouldn't have ... that must have cost a fortune.' Mum and Dad were both short of cash, so when Grandad splashed out they always protested. For me, it was yet more proof that Grandad loved me enough to buy me my favourite treats, but my parents didn't. I had no idea that grown-ups weren't all financially equal. His spending power became another tool of manipulation.

'Well, say thank you, then,' Dad said, pushing me towards his father. I inched towards him, gingerly hugging him. For a second it was as though I'd got my old Grandad back, and I wished beyond anything our physical contact could stop at these innocent hugs in front of all the family. He hugged me back, tight and whispered in my ear, 'You're my special little girl.' Then loudly, so everyone could hear, he told me to go upstairs and put my costume on. I skipped off, happier than I had been in a long time.

When I reappeared at the top of the stairs, I felt invincible. I'd taken my waist-length hair down, and it was held off my face by a proper golden headband. I clomped along in the big black boots, and swished the shiny red cape around until I made myself dizzy. 'This is the best birthday present ever!' I told Grandad, twirling round for him.

'I'd best be off in a minute,' my dad said after eating a slice of cake and washing it down with a cup of tea. 'Happy birthday, angel,' he said, kissing me on the forehead and preparing to leave.

As soon as he said goodbye, the fairy dust disappeared from my special day.

Gran was busy cleaning, preparing to go out, and Grandad read his paper.

I mooched onto the outside step, and sat, head in hands in my full Wonder Woman regalia. I hoped someone might walk by and notice my new costume, but the sun was almost down and a damp, dusky night was settling in, casting gloomy shadows. I walked over to the rock in the middle of the courtyard and surveyed my surroundings. I was an ancient Amazonian princess, and this was my spaceship I told myself. Standing on top of the rock, I jumped off to see if my cape would catch the wind and help me fly.

It didn't, but the neighbour across the way noticed me as she was shutting the curtains and waved, looking curiously at my outfit. I waved back, jangling my magical gold bracelet deliberately as I did, glad of the attention.

Bored, I went back and sat on the front step, ready in case someone might need the help of a superhero. 'Wonder Woman,' I sang to myself, listlessly.

'Come in for your tea,' Gran called out. I marched in, and stood, hands on hips, in a silly pose.

'You look great, love,' Grandad said, looking up and smiling.

As always, he was the only person who took the time to notice me.

Gran was putting my dinner in the oven, and I knew she'd be leaving soon.

I didn't beg her to stay, or feel resigned at what would happen to me when she was gone. It wasn't that simple. Instead, I just switched that side of my brain off completely. The part of me paralysed with fear, filled with shame and disgust, was banished to a faraway place inside me. I lived moment by moment. For this second, I was safe in my Wonder Woman outfit, with my gran nearby, and that's all my mind could deal with. People like to watch horror films to tantalize themselves with terror, but when your real life is a nightmare, you can't afford to play those games with yourself. So I tried not to think about what was about to happen to me.

With the curtains closed, the house seemed cosier than before. The fire was on, and I settled down in front of it to play with my toys. I was singing happily, and I pulled my hair back up in a ponytail so Grandad wouldn't be angry with me. I decided to draw a picture of myself in my new outfit. I drew stick legs and arms and an over-sized head, with what looked like orange flames shooting out to represent my hair. I was trying to get the gold belt right, without making it look like I'd chopped my body in half, when my life slipped into its evil alter ego and I was left alone with a monster.

'Bye, love.' I heard the door slam shut, Gran's voice trailing behind it. I looked up from my colouring book, my yellow crayon clutched tightly in my hand. Grandad must be upstairs. That was odd. As soon as we were alone, he usually ushered me straight to the bathroom, leering excitedly, as though he'd been anticipating this moment all afternoon. But I was alone for the moment. I smiled to myself, and part of me dared to dream. Would he not touch me this time? I wondered to myself, half holding my breath.

The telly was on, but turned down – it had been annoying Grandad earlier. Hearing it humming gently in the corner of the room just made the silence in the rest of the house more eerie. I glanced round, then went back to my colouring. I was just about to shade my cape in red when I heard his footsteps. They sounded different. Usually he clomped down the stairs with the certainty of a man in authority who has become arrogant in his actions. But his tread was more gentle, softly creaking on the steps as if he wasn't wearing shoes. I looked up anxiously. He appeared at the bottom of the stairs, like a revolting vision. His grey streaked hair was slick with Brylcreem, big strands congealed separately, and his hairy old feet were splayed out awkwardly, with dirty yellow toenails. He was wearing his dressing gown – *the* white robe. It had come to signal that bad things were about to happen to me.

His legs looked old and gnarled, they were mottled purple, laced with broken blue veins and dotted with brown liver spots. The skin on his knees was wrinkled and saggy. His body looked like a discoloured, baggy out-fit that had stopped fitting him properly any more. A shudder of disgust ran through me. I quickly looked back down at my picture. The best thing was to ignore him. I knew the consequences of staring at him, and didn't want him to say I was trying to get a closer look. But my heart pounded loudly.

He walked across the living room and sat in his special chair, in the corner of the room. It was a typical old man's chair, with a criss-cross tweedy pattern, and wooden arm rests. I kept my head down, focusing intently on what I was doing, but out of the corner of my eye I could see his hand moving up and down inside his robe. I was confused. When Grandad made me do that to him, I *hated* it. Why would he do it to himself?

I was so surprised at what he was doing I couldn't help but look, just to check it was really happening. It was like seeing someone doing something so strange you had to look twice to believe it was real. His dressing gown had slipped open, and his private parts, aged and wizened, were exposed.

He instantly seized on the fact that I had looked over.

'Come over and have a close look,' he told me, just like he usually did.

I thought about shaking my head, but I knew there was no point in disagreeing, so I reluctantly stood up and walked over.

'Kneel on the ground in front of me,' he said, and I recognized the tone of his voice, trying and failing to suppress his excitement. My legs were shaking as I knelt down in front of him, and I tried not to look straight ahead, as his penis poked outside his dressing gown in full view.

'This is a new game.' He smiled. 'This is the lollipop game.'

I sat there mute, not replying, and not knowing what to say.

He pointed at the tip of his penis – although I had no idea what a man called his parts back then – and said, 'It looks like the head of a lollipop doesn't it?' I turned my head away, and he put his hands on my head to make me look forward. 'Do you want to give it a lick?' he asked, smirking.

There was nothing in life I less wanted to do. The sight and smell of it was already making me feel sick, and the thought of getting closer to it made me want to retch. Grandad's chair was in front of the patio door, but the curtains were firmly shut, cutting us off from the garden and the world beyond it. I wanted desperately to cry out for help, but I knew it was pointless. The man about to hurt me was a member of my own family, and a paramedic.

No one would believe me – so I would have to endure it all alone.

I was seven years old. I was too young to watch films with sexual swear words, sexual content or violence. I couldn't leave the house on my own. I had only just learned to tie my own shoe laces and tell the time. I believed in Father Christmas, and I still left my teeth under my pillow for the tooth fairy to take. I had to stand on my tiptoes to reach the sink properly when I brushed my teeth at night, and my feet didn't touch the floor in the car. But here I was about to do something no child should even be able to conceive of, let alone be forced to do by a member of her family.

Grandad started to get cross when I wouldn't lick it, and changed tactics.

'Ouch, I've hurt it,' he said, looking pointedly at me. 'Why don't you kiss it better? You don't want me to be in pain now, do you?'

I was frozen with shock. I didn't want to, but other doubts were creeping into my mind. Grandad had made it clear what would happen to me if I wasn't a good girl.

Sensing my vulnerability and confusion, he pushed my head towards him, gripping his hands tightly round my ponytail.

My first reaction was to gag. The smell of tobacco on his hands was overwhelming, and he tasted old and musty – like when you walk into an old folks home. It was also desperately uncomfortable. Logic says that if you're a small child, with a tiny mouth, and an adult male is trying to force his parts in, it doesn't mix. At first he kept asking me to kiss the tip. But then he became more forceful, pushing me down. I was gagging and sobbing, trying to pull myself back, but the pressure of his hands on the back of my head meant I couldn't. The more excited he became the more he grabbed my head roughly, tugging on my ponytail and pushing me down further until I could barely breathe. Feeling like I was choking, I thought I might actually die, and I sobbed harder, tears splashing down my face.

As an adult, you understand the change in a man when he's about to ejaculate. But as a child you have no awareness of what's about to happen. Suddenly something vile filled my throat, choking me until I retched and retched as if I was trying to bring my insides up.

Then it was over, even though I didn't understand what had just happened.

'Clean yourself up, you're all in a mess,' he said gruffly, as I lay on the floor crying and gagging as I tried to stop myself from throwing up.

'You've got to stop being such a big baby. All grandads teach their granddaughters how to do this.'

My cape hung limply down my back as I climbed up the stairs and ran to the bathroom my throat burning and my stomach churning. I slammed the door and locked it, my fingers trembling with fear and shock. Snatching my toothbrush I scrubbed the inside of my mouth. Not just the teeth and gums, but all the way back to my tonsils. I scrubbed brutally until the blood dripped over my lips and tinged the bristles of the toothbrush bright pink. I didn't care. I just wanted to erase any part of him still left in my mouth. I wanted to feel clean again. But no matter how hard I scrubbed I couldn't take away the feeling that he had tainted me.

Every time I felt I'd learnt to cope with what was happening, the stakes got raised again.

What next? I wondered to myself, curling up in a tight ball on the bathroom floor, still wearing my Wonder Woman outfit. What would he do next?

My sobs reverberated round the bathroom, but no one heard them, and no one came to help me.

I was all alone.

5. Impossible Choice

'Sit down, we've got something to announce.'

My brothers and I sat in a neat line on the sofa, looking anxiously at Mum.

She was standing up, holding hands with her new partner, Neil. He was a large, friendly man, and although we didn't know him well, what we saw of him we liked. He reminded me of a big, cuddly teddy bear.

'We're getting married,' she said, beaming with delight.

There was a silence. It wasn't awkward; it was the quiet of kids trying to digest a new nugget of information that was slightly beyond them.

Even though I was eight by now, I wasn't grown-up enough to congratulate her, or leap up for a hug.

Instead we sat there slightly slack-jawed until Neil broke the silence, assuring us he wouldn't take the place of our dad. To be honest, that thought hadn't even occurred to me. *No one* could take the place of Dad, surely?

'Will you be wearing a big frock?' I suddenly piped up, remembering the wedding magazine I'd seen at the newsagent's, full of pictures of beautiful brides wearing frilly white dresses, looking like fairytale princesses.

Mum's smile widened and she looked towards Neil, squeezing his hand. 'Yes, we're going to have a proper white wedding,' she told me.

'Cool,' said Tom levering himself off the sofa, and picking up his football. It didn't matter to him if Mum got married or not, our parents had already divorced, and nothing could fix that. We already knew Neil was coming to live with us, and we'd be moving into a bigger house, so this news didn't make that much difference.

The boys sauntered out, and Neil joined them for a kick about. Mum stayed behind with me.

'Do you want to be a bridesmaid?' she asked, coming and sitting on the sofa with me, twirling my hair like she used to. I suddenly got an urge to throw my arms round her and confess what Grandad was doing to me. But I couldn't. Since her illness it caused Mum a lot of pain to be hugged. Because we didn't want to hurt her, we tried not to be too physical with her. During her illness I hadn't known what was wrong with her. All I knew was that she was sick and we couldn't be boisterous around her.

But six months in, I'd been snooping through Tom's personal belongings, trying to find the stash of Madness badges that he collected. Instead I'd found love letters from a girlfriend when he was twelve and had a revolving door of girls who he was besotted with, and who would write him silly little notes. Being curious, I decided to read them. After glancing through a few inane, lovesick ramblings, I came across a note that stopped me in my tracks. 'Sorry to hear your mum's got cancer,' it said. I knew cancer was a bad word, but I didn't know exactly what it meant.

The next time I saw Gran I asked her. 'What's cancer?' I said, trying to sound as casual as possible.

'Where did you hear that word?' she asked me sharply. I said I'd overheard Mum and Neil say it.

She sat me down, and picked her words carefully as she blew on her cup of tea to cool it down.

'It's a disease that makes things grow in people's bodies,' she explained, trying to keep it as simple as possible. 'If these things grow too big, they can take over and kill somebody.'

'Is that what Mum's got?' I asked nervously.

Deciding it was too late to lie, Gran confirmed my fears. 'Yes, your mum has got cancer, but they've cut it out and given her medicine to stop it growing back. She'll be fine – she's a strong lass.'

I gulped, terrified that Mum had things in her that had to be cut out.

Now I know she'd had a partial mastectomy and radiotherapy, and because of that she couldn't pick us up or give us a big hug. But at the time, I thought she just didn't love me much any more. I remembered her cuddling me all the time when I was younger. It seemed like another indication that Grandad was right – she had stopped loving me, and that was the reason I didn't get my night-time cuddle any more. He'd taken her cancer diagnosis and twisted it for his sick benefit. And I had been none the wiser.

So sitting on the sofa, desperate to give Mum a hug, all I could feel was this awful distance between us. I loved her, but I didn't know if I could trust her.

'I'd like to be a bridesmaid,' I answered her, reaching out my hand to touch her fingertips. 'What colour will my dress be?' I enquired. I'd inherited Mum's love of dressing up, fancy clothes and make-up, and she smiled.

'I don't know yet, but you can help choose it,' she said, reassuringly.

Then she left to find Neil, and I sat on the sofa thinking about the wedding.

That weekend, I announced to my grandparents that Mum was having a big white wedding and that I was going to be a bridesmaid. They already knew. That took the wind out of my sails a bit. I'd been looking forward to making the big announcement and showing off about the fancy frock Mum was going to buy me. Grandad always said that he and my parents discussed everything, and that they knew what he was doing to me – even if I couldn't mention what was happening. I thought it was our secret, so this confused me. But I knew I had to obey Grandad. As far as I was concerned, the fact he knew about the wedding before I did confirmed he wasn't lying.

The grown-ups discussed everything, even if I didn't know about it.

Out of the blue, Grandad started to talk a lot about what would happen when Mum got married, and we all moved to a new house.

He made a point of saying how terrible this would be for me, and how Mum loved me less than ever now. After our Saturday night ritual of abuse, he let me stay up to watch an hour of telly afterwards so he could talk to me.

By coincidence *Oliver Twist* was showing. When the scenes flashed up of Oliver at a mean-looking Victorian orphanage, Grandad commented that it was similar to the place where Mum wanted to send me. I stared at the screen in horror. It looked worse than prison. All the kids had to eat was bread and water. They couldn't play outside, and they were locked in cells for most of the time, looking miserable and alone.

'I'm worried that's where you'll end up after the move,' he said.

I'd not really thought much about where we'd move to with Neil. Since the divorce, it felt as though I'd had lots of homes, so it didn't bother me much. But Grandad was making a big deal about it. Before long, every other sentence would start with, 'after the move'.

'You'd be much better off living with your dad,' Grandad informed me one day. I looked surprised. No one had ever mentioned the possibility of staying with my dad before. He'd just moved into a police house, which looked like a fairytale castle, in a beautiful little village, with his girlfriend, Joan.

I didn't know her well, but we'd been out for drives into the countryside with her a few times. She tried really hard to be nice. Too hard. As kids, we winced at her ham-fisted attempts to win us over. It was as if she was trying to be our mum, and that didn't go down too well. But she seemed okay.

Other than Grandad, no one talked much about the move. It was all about the wedding. We didn't dwell on what would happen afterwards.

Then, Mum made another announcement. This time, it wasn't good news.

'You know that Neil's family are from Yorkshire, in England,' she began, as Tom and I propped ourselves up on the sofa. My youngest brothers Richard and Lee sat with Mum, looking oblivious to what was going on. 'Well, it's really hard for him to get a job up here, and he wants to be close to his family and friends.' She paused for a second. 'So we've decided to make a fresh start and move to England. It's your decision if you want to come with us.' She bit her lip nervously, and looked towards Tom and I.

There was no question of the two youngest boys staying behind.

The phrase, 'We've decided to make a fresh start,' stuck in my mind. It felt as though she wanted to leave her life behind, including us. Suddenly we weren't automatically included in the family 'we'. I felt abandoned.

Looking back, I wish that choice had not been placed in our hands. But as the two eldest children, Mum thought we were old enough to decide if we wanted to live with her or Dad. In my childish mind, I felt she didn't want us any more. The fact that she was prepared to leave us behind convinced me of that. I was eight, and all I'd ever known was life with my mum. I'd never imagined she could even contemplate life without me. It confirmed everything that Grandad had said to me.

It was a lot for a little girl to take in.

I'd already started seeing a child psychologist at school, on the recommendation of my teachers. Since the divorce I'd been behaving strangely, and they could see it had affected me badly. Of course, they had no idea what was *really* eating away at me, but they knew something was going on. I wasn't disruptive, but I'd changed from a normal, chatty, outgoing kid, to someone shy and withdrawn, who struggled to concentrate. I didn't really say much to the psychologist, Grandad had seen to that. As soon as he found out he pulled me aside and warned me: 'Don't tell them our secret or you'll be taken into care.' His look was the sternest I'd ever seen and I knew this was serious. So I just sat there and shrugged when she asked me questions about how I felt. They probably thought I was just another victim of the rising divorce statistics, and that I'd get over it when everything settled down.

It never once crossed my mind to confide in the psychologist. Grandad had such power over me, I just saw it as a test I had to pass by keeping quiet – to continue being his 'good girl'.

Now all these strands of misery were threading together into one big ball of pain. Mum was leaving, and it looked as if she didn't really want to take me.

'You don't have to make your minds up now,' she told us in a soothing tone, 'have a think about it and let me know.'

We nodded earnestly and both headed up the stairs for a conference. Bearing in mind we were only eight and thirteen, it wasn't the most adult of debates.

'Are you going?' Tom asked me, as we sat in his bedroom.

I shrugged, totally out of my depth. 'If we go Dad will be angry and if we stay, Mum will be angry ...' I mused, trying to weigh up the pros and cons. As I saw it, it was a no-win situation. Whichever way I looked at is, we were going to have to wave goodbye to one parent, probably for good.

I didn't want to upset Mum, but I *really* didn't want to upset Dad. If I made him cross, then Grandad would be angry with me too. Another big consideration was all the groundwork Grandad had laid for this very moment, which unbeknown to me, he had probably known about for weeks. 'Your mum doesn't want you – she'll end up giving you away.' His words rang in my ears, confusing an already difficult decision.

Tom stared intently at his *Star Wars* posters, as if Yoda was an oracle who might give us some clear guidance.

'I'm staying with Dad,' he suddenly announced. He didn't spell it out at the time, but when we discussed it later, he admitted that a driving force behind his decision was his not wanting Joan's sons to take his place.

Dad was also happily embracing a new family – and a fresh start. His job in the police force was going well, he'd moved into a picturesque family home, and his relationship with Joan was going from strength to strength. Like Mum, he was planning on remarrying. Joan already had two boys from a previous relationship, who were around Tom's age. We'd met them a couple of times on family outings, without realizing that the grown-ups were introducing us to each other to test the water for uniting us as a family. Being boys, there was a lot of competition between my brothers and Joan's lads. Tom, especially, wanted to make sure he was still Dad's number-one son. He felt threatened by this new addition to Dad's life, especially when he found out that Joan's boys were moving into the police house with them.

Because we lived with Mum, Tom was worried that Dad would forget about us. As it was, we visited at weekends, and Dad took us all out on family trips. But if we moved to Yorkshire, what would happen? He decided he needed to be with Dad to defend his place in the family, and make sure he wasn't usurped. My motivations were more complicated.

Because Grandad had never seen Tom as a threat, he'd never tried to poison me against him – all his efforts had focused on making me think my mother didn't love me. So when I realized Tom was staying, it tipped the balance significantly. I loved him, and he was one of the few people I believed still cared about me, other than Grandad. If I moved in with Dad, there was no chance I'd be taken to an orphanage – Grandad would see to that. Plus, Tom would be there as my playmate and companion. On the other hand, if I moved far, far away with mum I would be in real danger. It was obvious in my mind that she didn't really love me any more, so it was likely she'd get bored with me and send me away. But Grandad and Dad would be unable to save me. I wouldn't even have Tom to turn to.

'I'm going with you then,' I said firmly, my jaw set in place.

'Who's going to tell Mum?' Tom asked.

'You're the oldest, you should tell her,' I reasoned.

'So?' he replied, shrugging. 'You do it.'

We wandered down the stairs, nudging each other and giggling like naughty kids, not really aware of the gravity of the situation.

We couldn't face telling her, so we sat at the bottom of

the stairs, prodding each other and coming up with silly reasons why it should be the other who broke the news. It was such a big decision for little kids to make.

Eventually, Mum overheard us. 'So, have you decided then?' she asked, standing in front of us, hands on her hips, her face all tensed up.

Tom blurted it out, 'We're staying with Dad,' he said. I stared at the carpet, trying not to look at Mum's face.

'Right then, we'd better call your dad,' was all she said in response.

I was too young to interpret the tone of her voice, but she didn't beg us to change our minds, or give us reasons why it would be better to stay with her. Instead, she took it in her stride – further proof she didn't really care, to my mind. Around this time I do remember hearing her crying in her bedroom – the disconsolate sobs of someone really upset. I didn't think much about it. What with the divorce and ill heath, I'd got used to rows, tears and an atmosphere of sadness in the house. I didn't think this was any different. Many years later, Mum told me our decision 'broke her heart'. But she never gave us that impression at the time. Maybe we were too young to pick up on it, or she was too proud to show it. Either way, it marked a turning point in my life. Now I was moving to my dad's side of the family.

I was about to place myself in Grandad's clutches, with no chance of escape.

At first, the implications of my decision weren't obvious. That weekend we had a family meeting at Grandad's, where we discussed the new arrangements. I'd never seen him so happy. He was radiating excitement, and praising me continually, making more of a fuss than usual.

'See, I've taught you to be a good girl,' he told me, as soon as were alone together. 'You've made the right decision, you won't regret it.'

He continued to abuse me, but in a strange way, I'd got used to it. I still hated it, and it still left me traumatized and in terrible pain, but somehow I'd adjusted to it as a part of my life. My main concern was not being sent away.

I'd started to live two separate lives; it was like I'd got a twin. What happened to her was nothing to do with me. So when Grandad said how much fun I'd have at Dad's and that he'd take me canoeing, I was happy. I didn't stop and think of what lay in store for my other shadow side.

After some discussion my parents decided that it was best for us to both move in with my father straight away, rather than waiting until after the wedding.

It suited me just fine.

I was excited about moving in with Dad. His new house, the police station, was every child's fantasy. It had been originally built in 1805 and was made out of old red sandstone brick. Back then, Queen Victoria had made Scotland fashionable, and houses were designed to look romantic and impressive. The police house was a perfect example – it looked like something out of a fairytale, with a slightly sinister edge to it. There were turrets worthy of a princess, and narrow slits in the elaborate edging of the roof from where I imagined a prince might take his bow and arrow to defend his family. The village itself was small and quaint, steeped in history and folklore, with an ancient cemetery that legend said the devil had burned his claw marks into. The surrounding countryside was a beautiful medley of riverbanks, woodlands and green open fields, where you might easily stumble on a ruined castle or church, as you explored. Many paddocks had grand white horses grazing, and you could imagine the times when royals from ancient courts visited the area, galloping through the mists, through the forests and back to their ancestral homes. In more recent times, locals told tales of smugglers and pirates and, for young children, there was no shortage of legends to feed the imagination.

I felt I'd stumbled into my own wee fairy world, where anything was possible, and I could wander into the woods and be safe, with goblins, fairies and imps to watch over me.

To cope with what was happening to me, I often retreated into my own imagination, where I could create a fantasy world in my head. My new home was the perfect place to drift into dreams of other-worldly escape. Like any fairytale though, there was a villain – and soon, there would be a wicked stepmother too, just to make my misery even worse.

But when we first moved, there were no signs of what life would *really* be like. It was as if someone had drawn an idealistic portrait of family life and put me slap, bang in the middle of it. It felt like a fresh start for me, too.

The police station had three bedrooms. Dad and Joan shared one, and my brother and two new stepbrothers squeezed into another one. I had a room all to myself. I couldn't believe my luck. I'd never been so spoiled before – I even had my own TV. In the mornings I lay in bed, with the smell of the sea drifting in on the fog, listening to a family of blue tits chirruping outside my bedroom window. My bedroom wallpaper was 3D zigzag rainbows, which made you feel drunk as soon as you stepped in the room. It was an optical illusion, and if you stared at it long enough it looked as though the pattern was zooming out of the wall. I loved it, but any adult who came into my room soon left complaining of a headache. So it was my private space.

Downstairs, the house was more austere but still retained a cosy atmosphere. The carpets were plain brown, and the walls were painted a warm cream shade. There were antique mahogany furnishings, a soft grey velour sofa, and a beautiful open fire that roared with warmth on cold nights. A scuttle of coal sat by the fireplace to top it up when it ran low. The walls were lined with family pictures, including a large photograph of Great-granny Hobbs, whose eyes seemed to follow you around the room.

On our first evening together, everyone was on their best behaviour. We sat and ate dinner as a family, laughing at each other's jokes and making sure we didn't do anything wrong. Tom got on well with his new brothers, and they instantly fell in together, forming a clique. The change in family dynamics was odd for me. Suddenly I was the baby of the family again. I'd swapped two younger siblings for two older brothers. It felt good to be the youngest again, and I instantly became very clingy with Dad, acting like a baby scared to be left alone. But it *was* lonely. With three older boys forming an instant tribe together, I was left to my own devices.

After dinner, we all sat round the fire, Dad and Joan sipping from glasses of red wine, and us kids drinking juice and joking around. For dessert, we toasted chocolate on the open fire, piercing it on the end of an iron poker and taking it in turns to prod it into the fire. Compared to the uncertainty I'd just come from, I felt like life was about to get better. But I was wrong.

When our dinner had settled, Dad offered to take us on a tour of the house – including the police station underneath us. By accessing the house via the front door, you walked through the hallway straight into the house. But if you entered through the side door, you went directly into the police station, which even had its own cell. Being a quiet village, it wasn't often used.

By coincidence, the police cell was directly under my bedroom, a fact which Dad pointed out to me on my first evening there. He was just mentioning it as a point of interest, but I immediately bristled.

'Who gets put in the prison cell?' I asked cautiously.

'Bad people. But don't you worry about that,' he replied, tousling my hair and leading me down the stairs by the hand.

Bad people. Grandad was always warning me not to be bad. Is this what he meant?

'Do you want to look in the cell?' asked Dad, as we all trouped round the police station, which was cold, dark and slightly menacing.

'Yeah!' shouted the boys, excitedly. I was less sure . . .

He pulled out a set of big iron keys that looked like

something out of a Charles Dickens story. He jangled them jokingly, but the sound of them clashing together was ominous in my mind. The cell was old fashioned, with a rusty bike propped up in the back and proper iron bars at the front.

Tom pushed me forwards as I hesitated, reluctant to walk in.

As soon as all us kids were in, Dad slammed the door behind us, and peered through the bars locking the door as a joke.

'This is what happens if you're bad!' he told us in a mock-grave voice, messing around. The boys loved it, and were laughing hysterically.

I stood at the back trembling, consumed with absolute terror.

This was exactly what Grandad had warned me about.

Eventually, seeing the scared look on my face, Dad fumbled with the keys, and let us out. But we'd been locked in for a few minutes by then, enough time for me to solidify the idea in my mind that this could be my fate.

That night I tried to sleep, with the street lamp lighting up my room through the slit in the curtains. All I could think about was the police cell positioned directly underneath me. If I was bad, I'd languish to my death in there.

The next day Grandad came round to visit, more jovial than ever. My moving in with Dad had worked out perfectly for him. He could just drop round whenever he chose. No one would question him.

'How's life in your new home?' he asked Tom and me.

'Great,' we both replied in unison, with genuine gusto.

'They had a bit of a shock last night,' laughed Dad, nodding his head in our direction, 'I locked them in the police cell for a joke!'

'It was so funny!' Tom giggled. He thought it was cool that he could threaten his friends with jail if they started bugging him.

I stood by the fire in silence, biting my nails.

'The little bairn didn't like it though – she was scared out of her wits.'

Everyone looked at me, still laughing. Grandad smiled widely. Behind his smile I could see a scheming look in his eyes.

'You didn't like it in the police cell, then?' he asked, staring at me.

I didn't reply, but Dad answered for me, 'I told her that's what happens to bad girls, so she'd better behave!'

Grandad nodded in agreement, backing Dad up, but with none of his joking manner. Later on, he pulled me to one side, put his arm round my shoulder and whispered in my ear, 'See, if you're not a good girl for me, your daddy's going to put you in prison.'

I shuddered with fear.

He'd predicted that Mum would leave me – and he'd been right. Now, there was a new threat. If I didn't do as he said, I'd be put in prison. With the police cell just a few feet below my bed, it was a terrifyingly real possibility.

So began a new era of manipulation, torture and abuse.

6. Witch's Castle

'Surprise!' Dad was grinning with excitement as I walked through the door. I put my school bag down on the sofa and headed towards my brother, who was crouching on the floor in front of something.

'What is it?' I asked curiously as Tom, looking round at me with a beaming face, beckoned me over.

'It's a puppy,' said Dad, proudly. 'I bought it for you kids.'

I let out a sharp gasp, and raced towards Tom, dropping to my knees. Elbowing him out of the way, I saw a little ball of fur, cowering in the corner. The little pup was no bigger than my satchel.

'It's so cute!' I exclaimed, looking at the tiny border collie with wonder. I stroked it's fur, and then snuzzled my face into its fluffy neck.

'What's it called?' I asked, looking up.

'It's a she dog – and she hasn't got a name yet,' answered Dad.

'It's a little girl,' I said happily, looking back down into her chocolate-brown eyes. She yapped at me and wagged her tail for the first time.

Tom wandered off into the kitchen, looking disappointed it wasn't a boy. He joined our stepbrothers in the garden, who'd already tired of the new little addition to our family. Dad walked out after them and summoned them in for a family conference, annoyed with their indifference.

'Right, I bought this dog for you kids. You pestered me for it, and now it's entirely your responsibility. Between the four of you, you'll need to feed it, walk it and make sure it's well groomed. Me and Joan are too busy to get involved. Do you understand?'

We all nodded our heads in agreement. Having a dog to play with would be fun, although I could already tell that I would be the one in charge.

'So what are we going to call it then?' piped up Tom.

'It's a SHE – not an it,' I corrected him huffily.

Dad ignored me and told us that we had to choose the name between us.

'Rover!' shouted out David, our stepbrother.

'That's a boy's name!' I protested. Dad agreed, over-ruling the suggestion. For the next five minutes the boys volunteered a series of unsuitable names, all very masculine sounding. I couldn't get a word in edgeways to put forward my own ideas, which were at the other end of the spectrum.

Finally, Dad spoke up for me, 'Let Emily say what she thinks.'

'Jemima,' I said timidly, thinking what a pretty name it was.

This was greeted by spluttered protests from the boys.

'No way! What a poncey name,' said Tom, screwing up his nose.

'Kayleigh –' I had barely finished saying the name, before I was shouted down. I was a girly girl trapped with three boisterous teenage boys.

Suddenly I remembered one of my favourite television shows, and a genius idea popped into my head. 'What about Lassie? Like the dog off the telly.'

This name went down well. There was a murmur of general agreement, and Dad said, 'Okay, that's it then – she's called Lassie.'

And so I found my best friend.

At school I had no one to play with or confide in. I was a loner who found it hard to fit in with the other children. Maybe they sensed there was something different about me, and didn't like to be around me. But now I had my first real playmate.

I loved to walk along the riverbank, into the woods, stopping for a rest at the stream that picked its way through the leafy trees and mossy grass. After Dad's fantastic present, I was no longer alone on these jaunts. Lassie joined me on my epic walks, wagging her tail and sniffing every bush we walked past to check it was safe and no goblins would jump out at us – well, that's how I imagined it. She had a vendetta against squirrels and would rush off at top speed to try and catch one. I'd shriek with laughter as she dropped her front paws to the ground, wiggled her bum in the air and prepared to pounce. By the time she'd gone through her hunting ritual, the poor little squirrel would already be long gone up a tree. Lassie would fall in by my side again, looking despondent until the next creature caught her eye.

Back at home, she would leap up onto my bed, and pad round in a circle for ages before she finally settled into a comfy spot. I'd lie beside her, my head resting in my hands, and tell her all about my day.

After a while, I told her about what Grandad was doing to me.

'It's a secret,' I whispered into her furry ear.

Looking back it sounds silly – how can you confide in a dog? But at the time I really had no one I felt I could talk to. Just to have another creature near me, who listened silently to my stories, and could lick away my salty tears in sympathy, was a massive comfort.

Staying at the police station was not as idyllic at it had first seemed. I loved living in a fairytale house, I adored my new puppy and the beauty of our natural surround-ings, and it was great being with Dad. But my stepmother was about to become truly wicked.

I realized that there was competition between her and my mum, but I was too young to know just how bad it was. I later found out that during my mum's fight with cancer, Joan had visited her in hospital and whispered into her ear, 'Don't worry, if you die I'll have your children.'

She hadn't meant it in a kind, reassuring way.

Joan wanted my mother out of the picture, and for us to be classed as hers. Not because she loved us, but because she wanted to win the power struggle for Dad's kids – and his heart, as she saw it.

My father was a very traditional man. As far as he was concerned, it was his job to go out and earn the money, and the woman's job to raise the family. In Joan's mind, while we were living with her, we were her kids. Simple as that.

The problem was she didn't love Tom or me and favoured her two boys. It was like living in the *Cinderella* story. We would have to do all the worst chores, and if something went wrong, we'd be the ones to get the blame. If I tried to tell Dad what was happening, he'd wave me away and say it was Joan's business not his. So we were stuck with the old Wicked Witch of the West.

There wasn't a soft bone in that woman's body. She was a disciplinarian, who liked to enforce strict rules in the house – especially on me, who she saw as a second-class citizen and treated like an enemy.

Looking back, I imagine I reminded her too much of her arch rival – I was very feminine and girly, like my mum. Every time she saw Dad hug me, or say how much he loved me, it must have been like a dagger piercing her heart. She couldn't get to Mum, so she decided to break me instead.

Six months after I moved in, the day of my mother's wedding arrived – and Joan got her revenge. She was a dumpy creature with homely looks. Mum on the other hand was slight and pretty with perfectly groomed hair. All the talk of the wedding, and how beautiful Mum and I would look, must have twisted Joan's insides. I'd chosen a frilly polka-dot dress for my bridesmaid's outfit. It was so girly – like something Barbie might have worn. But at the time I loved it – calling it my princess dress. Mum, who had always loved my hair, planned to have it curled into ringlets and tied back off my face with pink ribbons. This was my big day – as well as my mum's.

I tried not to think about what would happen afterwards. Once she'd signed the marriage register, she would be walking up the aisle and out of my life.

For the moment, I focused on the happy times. Until Joan stepped in.

'Right, let's get you to the hairdresser,' she told me with a nasty look on her face, the day before the wedding.

I hesitated. Mum always sorted my hair out and took me to the hairdressers if it needed trimming. She was very particular about how much they cut off. Now, my hair had become a battleground for their power struggles.

'Mum's having a hairdresser come to the house tomorrow ...' I said, trailing off as I saw the stony look on Joan's face.

She didn't reply, and grabbed me by the shoulder, manhandling me out of the house and into the car.

'It needs cutting; it's such a mess,' she told me.

I couldn't protest. I was only eight, Mum wasn't around and Dad was too busy to worry about trivial things like my hair. Joan had total power over me.

In the hairdressers I sat there forlornly with a blue towel round my shoulders. My beautiful, long blonde hair hung down, almost touching my elbows. The hairdresser started to compliment me, but Joan butted in.

'It's all split, it looks like a dog's dinner. Cut it all off.'

I almost choked, letting out a strange strangulated sound.

Wielding the scissors, the hairdresser started snipping from the bottom, first an inch or so, until large tufts of hair were floating to the floor.

Trying to fight back the tears, I watched as my crowning glory was decimated. I was no longer a fairy princess – I looked like a boy.

Joan watched smugly, her arms folded across her expanding waistline.

'That's better,' she commented, with satisfaction.

'Do you want me to tidy up the back a bit more?' asked the hairdresser.

'Shave it,' Joan demanded.

I gulped as the electric shaver was switched on. The high-pitched buzzing sound and the rough touch of the metal on the back of my neck was awful.

Afterwards, the hairdresser took out a mirror and showed me the back and sides. I'd got a severe pageboy cut, with the nape of my neck shaved. I was too shocked to say what I really thought. Instead I mumbled my thanks, and sat in silence as Joan drove us home, looking very pleased with herself.

The morning of the wedding was carnage. Mum's yell was louder than the church bells when she saw what Joan had done to my hair.

'How *could* she?' Mum screamed, flying into a raging hissy fit at Dad, who had dropped me off. He just shrugged it off. To him, it was just hair.

I stood by miserably, thinking how stupid I'd look in my princess dress with a horrible boy's haircut. The whole day was spoiled for me – and Mum. But what could she do? I no longer lived with her, and she was about to get married and move to another country, starting a new family. When Joan had my hair cut she also, symbolically, cut my bond with my mother. At this moment, it became evident whose family I now belonged to.

*

With Dad busy at work most of the time, the two adults who had most control over me now were Joan and Grandad. It felt like they had both dedicated their lives to making my life a misery. I was in big trouble.

Taking advantage of all this family disruption, Grandad decided to upscale his abuse. So far he'd been cautious, stealing moments when we were alone and he thought he could get away with it. His attitude to me had been manipulative rather than downright threatening. When I sobbed as he hurt me, he never stopped, but he did try and soothe me. Now all that changed. It was as if he'd let his guard down. When I lived with Mum, he feared I might tell and that she would believe me. But with Dad – his own son – in charge of me, he felt much more in control of the situation. He knew he could fob my father off if I decided to confess what was going on.

Everything about Grandad changed towards me from his tone of voice to his taunts. He also became far more sexually aggressive. During the grooming, he'd acted like the child catcher in *Chitty Chitty Bang Bang* – trying to lure me into his trap with sweets, pretty words and promises. Now, it was as if the cage door had slammed shut, and he didn't have to pretend any more. He treated me like an object for his pleasure – at any cost. If I cried or tried to pull away in pain, he'd twist my arms roughly behind my back to pin me down, or pull my hair violently to make me comply.

It's hard to describe the immeasurable difference between someone who is hurting you, but appears to want to minimize your pain in some way, and someone who no longer cares about what you're feeling or what damage they might be doing. It multiplies the fear and panic by a million.

Because of Dad's job, there were still plenty of opportunities for Grandad to spend time with me. He often volunteered to babysit when my father was doing extra shifts and Joan was too busy to bother looking after me.

The 'games' Grandad made me play were getting more obscene by the day. Now he was assured that I was his to abuse, he'd become creative. What he did to me next was more painful and degrading than I could bear.

'I'm training you to be a woman,' he told me the first time it happened.

Of course, I didn't understand what he meant. I was too young to realize that he was literally trying to prepare me for future attempted rapes.

The seed was first planted when we went shopping in a local supermarket, Grandad pushing the trolley as Gran loaded it. I trailed behind, skipping forward haphazardly every now and again, tapping my fingers against the cold metal handle. Every so often I'd pipe up, asking for sweets and pink wafer biscuits. Gran would shake her head as Grandad slipped them in, winking at me indulgently. It was always the same to the outside world; I was his little princess. But they couldn't see inside him like I could.

That shopping trip was the first time I noticed the glint in his eyes as Gran picked up a cucumber, appraising it to see if it was the right size and ripeness. Suddenly, under his grinning gaze its shape seemed lewd and embarrassing. Really, for a child my age I shouldn't have even been able to make that connection. It should have always been just an innocent vegetable. But I'd seen too much – known too much – to see the world through such naive eyes. As the cucumber was placed in the trolley, Grandad gave me such a knowing leer that I shuddered. Even though I was aware enough to click that something was amiss, and that it was linked to 'our little secret', I still couldn't work out exactly why. But I would soon find out.

That evening, with the house empty of the people who could protect me, Grandad introduced a new, frightening element into his repertoire of abuse. He began using objects on me. At first it was vegetables, like the cucumber Gran had innocently purchased that afternoon. Later it would involve other items stolen surreptitiously from the fridge, until eventually he would use anything he could lay his hands on – from brush handles to the pens and pencils I used to scribble childish drawings of my home and my dog. Stick people, stood outside a house outlined in red with a yellow sun in the sky and a rotund dog on the path. I sobbed, begged him to stop. But he wouldn't. Soon I spent every moment in fear. I'd be skipping across the living room, singing loudly, creating fantasies in my head, when suddenly I'd find myself thrown across the arm of the sofa. My head pushed into the suffocating depths of the velour cushions, barely able to breathe, as he introduced a new object into 'our games'. Unlike fingers, which are flexible, these objects were hard, unrelenting and capable of terrible damage to a little girl.

Grandad had a solution for everything though. He'd

taken to buying a fresh pack of knickers for me every week. After the abuse was over, I'd hand over my blood-soaked knickers to him, clean myself up as he instructed, then pull on a brand new clean pair.

I never know how he disposed of the evidence of his terrible deeds.

He was more machine than man. He looked at my pain and misery through logical eyes not human ones. My body was either an object for his pleasure or a problem that needed to be solved. It felt as if it didn't belong to me any more, as though it was someone else's suit that I slipped on and off at will.

What I remember more than anything was the terror at the escalation of what was happening. Something monstrous in him wasn't satisfied by anything he could do to me. These weren't sexual acts – they were sadistic acts of torture. My pain wasn't a by-product of his pleasure – it had started to become the *focus* of his pleasure. So to get his hit, he had to hurt me more.

At eight years old I couldn't explain this feeling. I just *knew* it.

This was beyond the sexual relationship consenting adults might have – and with a young girl who was too scared to say no. It was a force of evil.

There had also been another terrifying development. The abuse had always happened in the depressing confines of Grandad's house before, but soon he felt confident enough to abuse me anywhere. He'd drive me round, searching for secluded spots where he could force me to play our games.

'Want to feed the horses?' He'd chuckle, brandishing a

bag of carrots Gran had helpfully given to him, unaware of their true purpose.

When we set out on our little adventures, he'd taken to telling her that we were going to feed the horses. The area was an equestrian hotbed, and most fields were filled with pacing horses, grateful to munch on a carrot snack, fed to them by an excited young kid accompanied by a loving parent or grandparent.

'Take these, then,' she would say, pressing a bag of leftover carrots into his hands, unaware he was trembling with excitement.

Needless to say, the carrots never made it to their intended destination. Instead they were used on me – used to torture me.

He'd also found a terrifying new spot to abuse me in this way – known locally as the Witch's House.

Our first visit took place after a few months at my new home. Grandad picked me up after school, still wearing his paramedic's uniform. He'd come straight from work, and he was agitated and excited.

'We're going to a special place,' he told me, driving along the narrow country lanes. It was dusk and the trees cast haunting shadows across the road, a lingering fog hung over the nearby loch. As we approached our destination, the roads became more deserted; as it became rare to see another car pass by, I started to tremble with fear.

'Here we are,' he told me with a grimace, pulling into a parking space hidden behind the bushes. 'Do you want to have a look around?'

I didn't, but as usual I blindly obeyed, following him as

he strode towards an imposing Gothic gateway, which towered over the road. The bases of the arches were overgrown with ivy, twisting round them and almost completely covering the large black-trimmed heavy stones.

I shivered. The night was drawing in, the temperature had plummeted. I was still wearing my school uniform, and the little jacket wasn't that warm. My grey flannel skirt only reached my knees and there was a gap between where it ended and my white, knee-high school socks began.

We must have looked a strange sight. An old man, over six feet tall, wearing a paramedic's uniform, walking alongside a tiny little girl dressed in her school uniform. The fact we were heading towards an abandoned house, at dusk, would have looked even odder to a passer-by, but no one was around to witness what was happening. Grandad grabbed my hand, pushed the gate open, and led me up the path; a tumble of plants, pebbles and the fragments of old debris lay about.

As we approached the forbidding, abandoned old country house, I shivered with fear. It was silhouetted against the darkening lilac sky, watching over us as we walked into the deserted grounds. I'd heard rumours about a scary haunted house deep in the countryside near my village. Now I was here, at nightfall. To me, it looked exactly like the castle from the *Wizard of Oz*, where the Wicked Witch of the West imprisons Dorothy. It was a nightmarish place for a little girl with a big imagination.

In reality, it had been the grandiose home of a Scottish shipping tycoon at the turn of the last century, when architecture was dramatically Gothic. Like the police house where I lived, it represented the height of elaborate, romantic building popular at the time. To modern eyes this style has an almost fairytale quality, with sinister undertones of long-gone lives. But there was something even more disturbing about the design of this particular house – a collection of stone statues of monkeys, scattered round the grounds like evil incarnations. As my eyes focused on their shadowy shapes, my heart pounded even faster. It was exactly like the scene from the *Wizard of Oz*, with the witch's evil monkeys slithering all over the castle to capture their prey – a little girl.

The original owner had been fascinated with all the exotic creatures he'd encountered on his many travels across the globe – especially the monkeys he'd discovered in Asia. When he returned to the grey skies of Scotland, he'd wanted a reminder of the amazing things he'd seen on his trips, so he decided to commission hand-carved reproductions of the sinewy monkeys and have them cast in stone to decorate his Gothic mansion. It was an eccentric addition to an already imposingly ornate house.

Now abandoned, the carved statues gave the place a creepy, surreal atmosphere. Many of the stone monkeys were attached to the brickwork of the house, as if they were creeping up the sides to get in, their long tails curled round pipes and drains to support themselves. Some were standing in the garden, their movements frozen as if they'd been caught trespassing.

'Are the monkeys real?' I stuttered to Grandad, looking up towards the house.

He sniggered, clutching my hand tighter and dragging me along the path.

'An evil witch has put a magic spell on them, so they can't move.' He laughed, holding my wrist until it hurt.

I gulped. My worst fears had been confirmed. It definitely was a witch's castle and she probably already knew I was here and was out to get me. It's hard to say what I was most frightened off: the evil, despicable crimes I knew Grandad would inflict on me, or the terrifying prospect of mysterious tortures an evil witch might perform with her dark spells. Sadly, for a little girl, the fear of the unknown is always more sinister.

What my grandad was doing was unspeakable, but at the same time he had promised to take care of me when no one else wanted me. The fear of how bad life could get was more threatening than how bad it actually was. It was this childish reasoning that Grandad twisted to manipulate me into silence.

'If you're a bad girl, the witch will turn you into stone too,' he added, as we walked past a monkey, tortuously twisted into a locked shape, 'so you'd better be good.'

I nodded, and clung to his side. It was hard to know who was the enemy any more. Any points on a moral compass were spinning out of sight.

Just before we reached the house, Grandad found an upturned stone and sat down to roll a cigarette. I knelt down by his side and watched as he licked the paper to seal it and tapped the end to tighten the tobacco. He took slow, leisurely drags and looked into the distance. He was savouring the moment, as I trembled with fearful anticipation by his side.

'Have you enjoyed our little outing?' he asked, looking

down at me with a half smile, his fingers twisting a lock of my hair tightly.

I shrugged first, then nodded vigorously as I saw a cloud of annoyance pass across his face. 'Yes, thank you,' I added for good measure.

'Well, it's not over yet,' he leered.

Would he hurt me here? I wondered with fear, shivering in the damp, cold air. As every minute ticked by the temperature seemed to drop.

'How about we go and feed the horses?' he said, standing up suddenly.

My heart sank fifty fathoms below sea level.

I knew exactly what that meant. I looked at the sky, searching for a wicked witch on a broomstick. The thought wasn't as scary now, and part of me hoped she'd fly by to save me. But all I could see was the distant spotlights of faraway stars, and the odd silver streak of a plane shooting across the sky.

We walked back along the overgrown path, with Grandad's pace quickening at every step. Visiting the house had just been another tool to manipulate me.

Now he'd convinced me my mum didn't want me, he had to use other tricks to scare me into believing his horrible lies. He knew I had a vivid imagination, and he played on it to control me. I was still young enough to believe in fairies, witches and magic spells. Seeing the monkeys frozen in time was another way to warn me of what might happen if I didn't do as I was told. He knew what he was about to do to me – and how much I hated it.

We headed for the warmth and supposed safety of

the car so he could carry out the evil deeds he'd been planning all along.

By the time we crossed the road, it was pitch black – but I could still see the house against the skyline. Its presence was like a warning.

Grandad opened the car door and pushed me into the back seat. As I pressed my tiny face against the cold glass of the car's window I mouthed 'Help' into the darkness. I knew no one could see, but it made me feel better. Like the stone monkeys, I was trapped. Now, with visions of bewitched monkeys whirling in my head, I let the tears trickle down my face, mirroring the rain that had started to slide down the outside of the car's window panes. I watched in silent agony as the clouds raced across the night sky, playing hide and seek with the moon, occasionally highlighting the horrors of the Witch's House over on the hill.

I closed my eyes on Grandad's gloating, gleeful grin as he ordered me into position. He'd got it all planned out.

Like the monkey's hidden in the darkness, I felt myself turn to stone. An evil spell it would be hard to break.

7. Please Not That

It's sad to admit, but I can't remember the day my mum left. She just slipped out of my life, changing into another woman with a new family to love and look after. Our relationship had been dismantled piece by piece, like a jigsaw missing so many bits you can't remember the picture any more.

First she was my world, the person I relied on for everything in my life. Then after the separation she became someone who had a life outside being my mum, and I felt slightly pushed out in the way kids do. Then she got cancer, and suddenly she was someone fragile and sick, who I could easily lose. When I moved in with Dad, she faded into someone I only saw on weekends, day trips or holidays. She became a casual visitor in my life.

I still loved her, but our worlds weren't linked together as intimately any more. Our relationship was dissolving.

After the wedding, Mum moved to Yorkshire and left for good.

There were no dramatic goodbyes. We'd visit, I'd spend holidays there – that was how the grown-ups had put it, as if it wasn't something permanent. But I missed her like crazy. Well, I missed the *idea* of her.

When I lost my mum, I lost a grip on anything resembling normality. She became a figment of my imagination

– and all the proof I needed that Grandad was right. He'd predicted she'd leave me, and she had.

I'd taken to telling lies to fabricate the kind of family life I imagined everyone else was living. Building a dream existence out of fragments of memories and snatched conversations of other kids was the only way I survived. My life became a story I told myself. It wasn't real, because the reality was so terrible my young mind couldn't cope with it.

'I went to the cinema with my parents last night,' I'd tell any kid who would listen. It was all fiction. We didn't do anything as a family. Now there was no need to win Tom and I over, all pretence at nice days out together were done away with. Dad took his job as a policeman very seriously. He worked all hours, and there was no time for frivolities. Family niceties weren't Joan's style either – not for us stepkids, in any case.

I'd often get caught out in my stories. Before long I got a reputation in the village as a liar. It drove Joan mad. She thought it brought shame on the family. One day I made the mistake of telling a teacher I'd been to a New Kid's On the Block concert. I'd heard the other children talking about it, and I stole their anecdotes as my own. The teacher mentioned it at parents' evening as a way of making casual conversation. Of course, Joan had no idea what she was talking about, and it was a really awkward moment

The next night, straight after school, she dragged me up the stairs, pulling my hair viciously.

'WHAT'S WRONG WITH YOU??' she screamed. 'Are you trying to make me look like an idiot?'

I shook my head vigorously.

'You need to be taught a lesson.'

She pushed me over the bed and struck me with the buckle end of the belt.

I flinched, and let out a cry.

She struck me again, even more violently.

This time I choked back my sob.

It only made her angrier.

'I don't know what's wrong with you,' she yelled as she lashed out.

The less I responded, the more she lashed me with the belt; she was out of control. To me this was nothing. I'd take a thousand lashings with the belt rather than what Grandad made me endure, so her violence was futile. Joan couldn't break me. Someone had already got there before her . . .

Afterwards, I crept out of the house and made my way to my favourite hiding place – the cemetery. It might be a morbid place for a young girl to hang out, but I didn't fear the dead. It was the living who scared me. The silence and solitude among the graves was the closest to tranquillity I got. The old grey stones jutted out from the ground at awkward angles, as if the earth was trying to spit them back out. The cemetery had originally been the burial place for plague victims, but since then had become a final resting place for locals. Walking up the lane, I took in the familiar sights and relaxed slightly. The cemetery was divided in two by a road, still old fashioned by modern standards, winding through the greenery with only room for one car to pass. They seldom did though. Other than the faint sounds of car engines humming in the distance and the caw of seagulls overhead, it was silent.

At the intersection of the road, before you turned left to the church – still a lynchpin of the community, not a relic like in some places – a large, discoloured wall loomed over the road, signalling the start of the graveyard. This spot was infamous in the area. Legend had it that the devil had tried to break into the grounds, pressing its clawed hand into the wall to launch itself up. But as soon as its demonic claw touched the stone, which was hallowed ground, it let out an inhuman scream and was thrown backwards. All that was left of its attempt to steal into the cemetery was the imprint of its three claws, burned for ever into the stone. To this day you could see the three indentations in the brick work. Who knows where it really came from, but as kids, we took the legend as gospel.

As usual, I stopped to trace my small fingers tentatively in the large dents. I shuddered at the thought of the devil trying to violate the grounds. But I also felt reassured it had been barred from entering. It confirmed in my mind that this was a safe place, where evil was banished.

I tripped over the remains of three white candles at my feet as I walked, the wax frozen like molten lava into the grass. People still came from all over to perform rituals here, but I was too young to understand what they were for.

Innocently, I ambled along, turning left into the oldest part of the cemetery.

I glanced at a stone as I walked past and saw the date, 1788, and the name Mary. I couldn't work out if that was the date of her birth or her death. In the distance the fading sun was shimmering over the banks of the river. There were still a few hours of light left, and with my legs starting to throb from my thrashing, I pulled back a draping curtain of ivy and made my way into a little den, hidden from sight. It must have once been a tomb, because names and dates were inscribed on stones embedded into the tumbledown brick walls. But nature had claimed it back as her own now. Damp green moss carpeted the floor and obscured much of the brickwork. The roof was patchy and pieces of cloudy blue sky peered through. I settled myself down on a large rock towards the back of the space and curled up into a ball, my head tucked between my knees, and my arms embracing my legs tightly into my body. Now I could allow myself to cry. The tears splashed down my face feverishly, as I rocked backwards and forwards in a comforting movement.

'Why does Joan hate me so much?' I sobbed to myself.

I really couldn't understand what I had done to deserve everything that was happening to me. But I started to believe I must have done *something* wrong. Why had Mum left me? Why did Joan hit me and call me a liar? Why did I have no friends at school? Why did Grandad hurt me so badly . . .

I was basically a good kid, even if I did have my head in the clouds. I couldn't work out why life was working out so badly for me. At home, when I was playing with Tom and my new brothers, I could be cheerful and outgoing, singing along and putting on shows for them. But as soon as I got outside my front gate I turned in on myself with shyness. None of the children at school liked me. It wasn't that they *disliked* me – they just looked through me as if I didn't exist. I didn't know how to talk to them or fit in. My life, behind closed doors, was so different from theirs. I often felt we were living in parallel worlds and were from entirely different species.

Dad would sometimes pick me up from school in his police car, and for a moment I'd feel proud of the family I came from. I'd see the other kids throw envious glances in my direction as he strode around in his uniform. They probably thought I was stuck up, thinking I was above playing with them because my father and his father were important men in the community. Grandad would sometimes wave as the ambulance roared past the playground, and people would whisper, 'She's his granddaughter.'

But mostly, I was a solitary figure at the school gates, watching as other mums fussed over their children, wrapping their coats round them more warmly and making sure they'd eaten their packed lunches. It was only a short walk home, but every step was a knife in my heart, knowing I was alone.

The only person who greeted me enthusiastically on my return was Lassie. She'd wag her tail so hard it would become invisible and rub her warm nose all over my face as a delighted greeting when she saw me.

I still idolized Tom but he'd fallen in with his step-brothers to form their own gang. They were tough teenage boys, who liked to prowl around and have a laugh. What could they have in common with a strange, intro-verted eight-year-old girl, who liked to sing and dance?

Sighing, I wiped my nose and took out my drawing

book from my satchel. It was cold out, but the tomb I was sheltering in was protected from the worst of the winds, and felt as safe and comforting as it was likely to get.

When I felt sad, I liked to doodle in my book and write poems. I didn't write about what was happening to me – I didn't know what words to use, and I was too scared of anyone finding it. Instead, I created an imaginary world, drawing princesses and white horses that galloped through yellow meadows. We'd learned in history class that Lady Jane Grey had visited the area, and I wrote a small song about her adventures, picturing her in a fine blue velvet dress, with sleeves that spread outwards into elegant points.

My hair had started to grow back after my ordeal at the hairdressers. Now Mum was gone, Joan couldn't be bothered worrying about it any more. I could feel it tumbling down my back, and I shook my head imagining I was Rapunzel throwing down my long tresses. Usually I packed a sandwich on my little visits to the cemetery, but tonight I hadn't had the chance. Only the gnawing in my stomach drove me back home – plus the thought of Lassie snuggled under the dining table.

Musical ability ran in our family. My auntie was a singer, and my grandad could play a fair few instruments and carry a tune. I hated to think that I took after him or his family line in any way, but I had the musical gift too.

At school, performing was the only time I really shone. When it came to plays and concerts, I was always in the lead role or sitting proudly at the front of the orchestra.

I'd recently taken up playing the violin, much to Joan's annoyance. 'Stop making that racket – it sounds like someone's dying!' she would scream up the stairs at me as I practised. I tried to ignore her and carry on. Most of the other children's mothers encouraged them, but I had to be my own inspiration. Grandad took some interest in my talent too.

On the nights when he'd given me a reprieve, or most likely, before his sexual attacks had begun, he'd play country music in the lounge. He'd tap his knee in time to the music and sing along over the top. He loved Johnny Cash, and the singer's dark, sonorous tones would envelop the house. I didn't understand the lyrics, but I felt they were coated in pain. Grandad enjoyed singing along, but something about the songs made me feel melancholy. I preferred the female country and western singers, who sounded as though the bad times hadn't beaten them yet. They were upbeat and honest, singing about survival and hoping for happier times. Their attitude struck a chord with me, and I'd happily warble along over the top, giving it my all to reach the high notes. Grandad clapped along encouraging me, and I'd play Dolly Parton to his Kenny Rogers, duetting together about being islands in the stream. In these moments, everything else ceased to exist. There was just me and the music. It was the best balm I ever found. But even in these snatches of innocent amusement, Grandad was plotting against me, planning how to turn my pleasure into his own.

'Go upstairs and try your gran's clothes on,' he'd say encouragingly. I loved dressing up so I didn't need any persuading. In a flash I'd bolt up the stairs and start riffling through her wardrobe. After a few moments, I'd appear at the bottom of the stairs and strike a pose, my high falsetto belting out the words to 'Jolene', not really understanding what they meant. I'd be a comical sight, wearing high heels a million sizes too big for me – so large I'd have to drag my feet along the floor to walk. All my gran's dresses were dowdy and sensible, so Grandad shouted upstairs that I should put on one of her under-slips. They were white and skimpy, hanging off my body. I'd tie a knot in the straps to keep them up, often tripping over the hem with my grown-up heels and ending up in a giggling ball on the floor. Grandad laughed along too, and for a second I saw a shadow of the man I'd loved so much. But he was long gone. I was just a kid who loved dressing up, but Grandad's interest was far more sinister.

Seeing me like this planted another perverted idea in his mind. He didn't have the nerve to carry out his new plan yet, but it was only a matter of time. I carried on performing for him, unaware of what he was hatching. I couldn't imagine he was secretly fantasizing about dress-ing me up in adult stockings and suspenders, wondering when he could satisfy his sick dreams.

Of course, unless it was a private performance Grandad wasn't interested in my achievements at school. Unless there was some perverse kick in it for himself, my abilities meant nothing to him as I soon found out.

The months had sped by since I first moved into the police house, and it was now December. I struggled to find something to celebrate this Christmas.

Walking through the village, I pulled my hand-knitted scarf tight, trying to ignore the bobbly hat on my head that Gran had made for me to a pattern that had fortunately died with the seventies. Even the crisp air had undertones of festivity to it. It was cold, but in a Christmassy way.

For Dad, everyone else's revelry meant more hard work for him. We even had a few drunks locked up in the cell for the night too refreshed to make their way home or set on disturbing the peace. I could hear them slurring through the best known carols as I lay in bed.

Tonight was the opening night of the school nativity play and I had a starring role. Literally. Decked out in a massive silver-foil costume, I was to play the star of Bethlehem, serenading the new baby Jesus with my very own singing solo – added especially to showcase my voice.

I'd been rehearsing for weeks, both at school and in the privacy of my bedroom. 'SHUT UP SQUAWK-ING!' had been Joan's only response to the good news about my upcoming role. But Dad was impressed, and took to calling me his 'little singing star', which only served to annoy Joan even more.

But on the night of my triumphant performance no one accompanied me to the school, and I set off alone. Both Dad and Gran were working, Joan would rather drink arsenic than see my glorious moment, and Grandad couldn't be bothered to turn up. He didn't like seeing me in public – I couldn't be his 'special' girl.

As I set off, I turned back and looked at the house. An ornate, Victorian lantern was beaming cosily over the porch, and through the closing door I caught a glimpse of the sparkling Christmas tree and the roaring coal fire. From the outside, my life looked like a scene from a greeting card.

But as I trudged through the village alone, practising my words, it was far from the truth. I turned into the village hall, next to the church, only to be blinded by the headlights of proud parents arriving to see their children.

An hour later I stood on the stage, wedged inside a silver-star costume, singing my heart out to the audience. I scanned their faces, looking for someone I knew. But none of my family were there to witness my success. Afterwards, a few of the teachers congratulated me as I lingered backstage, trying not to let the bitter taste of disappointment taint my big moment. I could see mums rushing to hug their little darlings, telling them how clever and talented they were. I hung around for a few moments longer, and then decided to set off back home. No one even noticed me slip out.

I bunched my hands deep into my pockets as I walked along the street. It was only a few minutes, and perfectly safe for me to be alone, but that wasn't the point. If I disappeared, no one would even notice, I thought to myself bitterly. The decorations made every home look inviting as I passed by on the way to the police house, where I lived.

Joan didn't ask about the play. She just pursed her lips and did her chores. When Dad finally made it home, he made a big fuss, and asked me to tell him word for word what had happened. As I sat on his knee, explaining how my costume was made, I wished more than anything he'd been there.

But then it was bedtime, Dad was tired and needed to eat his dinner.

'He's been hard at work all day,' said Joan, with a reproachful tone.

She didn't say it, but her every gesture suggested that he wasn't really interested and was just being polite. I knew Grandad would have agreed.

Later that night, I lay awake in bed looking at the stars through my window. I'd be nine soon. I should be excited about growing up. But Grandad had ruined that. 'You'll be all grown-up soon,' he said with a glint in his eye. Being grown-up was bad, that's all I knew for sure.

I was staying over at his house the next night, and fear consumed me just as absolutely as sleep. No one cared about me – tonight had proved that.

I was slipping deeper into his clutches.

Over the next year Grandad played on my feelings of loneliness to continue grooming me. As the seasons changed, the only continuity in my life was his terrifying abuse. Every time I thought it couldn't get worse, it did – his sadistic attacks with objects would be more frequent, and more savage.

By the following Christmas his behaviour towards me had become almost reckless. The difference between the two masks he wore – one for me, and one for every-one else – was becoming more shocking by the minute. Every day I contemplated the vast chasm between the respectable paramedic everyone loved and the monster

I knew. At Christmas, Grandad was the centre of the community; he raised money for charity, made sure needy kids had nice presents. He was treated like a saint.

Today was the big day of festivities in the village, and I slipped my best jumper on – knitted white snowflakes on a background of rainbow stripes. It was hard to tell if the butterflies in my stomach were down to the excitement of Christmas or fear of spending the day with Grandad.

Even though I was lonely, Christmas was still a magical time for me. I left a nip of whisky and a mince pie out for Santa, and I always set aside carrots for Rudolph the reindeer. I could separate myself off from the horror of 'feeding the horses' – it was the only way for me to survive. Despite what Grandad was doing to me, the core of me still connected to true childish innocence was intact. I could feel the inherent 'goodness' of Christmas, and I loved it. Everyone was happy and jolly – even Joan was grudgingly cheerful around the house. The sparkle and glittery razzle of the decorations strung up on the streets, in school and in the house filled me with joy. On cold nights I could hear the faint voices of carol singers brought over on the wind, or the church choir would break into song outside the front door, gladly accepting a slice of Christmas cake as thanks. I'd warble 'Silent Night' in front of the fire, and for once my stepmother wouldn't snarl at me to shut up. We even put tinsel on the top of Dad's police hat for a joke, and he tickled me as a punishment.

Compared to other kids I knew, these were only snatched moments of happiness. But they were all I had, so I made the most of them.

The village fete was held in the church hall. There were stalls filled with charity Christmas cards, home-baked cakes and trinkets for sale. A cranky cassette recorder played a greatest hits compilation, and old ladies wearing gold tinsel at jaunty angles on their heads sang along to 'I'm Dreaming of a White Christmas', while serving up hot cups of tea in white Styrofoam cups.

Within minutes of arriving, Joan was off chatting to a neighbour, and I was directed towards Santa's Grotto. I wasn't sure if I still believed in Father Christmas, but I liked the myth, and was happy to go along with it. All the kids were chattering excitedly in the queue as I took my place in the line. I couldn't wait to get a present.

Suddenly it was my turn. The innards of the grotto were dark, lit up only by red and pink fairy lights, making everything look mystical. Santa grabbed me and sat me on his knee. His beard felt like cotton wool on the side of my face, which tickled my face and made me want to laugh. His scarlet red costume was reassuringly familiar, but something inside me felt instantly uncomfortable. I wanted to get my present and go.

'So have you been a good girl?' he asked, leaning towards me.

I winced at the question, feeling I might pass out. The voice sounded oddly familiar, and there was a knowing intonation to Santa's words.

I squirmed on his knee, trying to get off. But he put his arms round me and pulled me closer, and whispered in my ear, 'Or have you been bad?'

His breath smelled of rotten tobacco and decay. I shuddered. Suddenly I was overcome with an urge to burst into tears. I scrambled off his lap, grabbed the gift a surprised pixie was proffering, and bolted out of the grotto.

My heart was beating at double speed. Was it a conspiracy? I was too young to make the connection. It never occurred to me it actually *was* Grandad. I still assumed that if Santa did exist he lived in Lapland, surrounded by snow. He couldn't be someone I knew – that was impossible. But it felt like an evil, oppressive presence was closing in on me, always speaking those same words: 'Are you a good girl?' It was said in such a way to instantly make me feel bad, as if there were some unspecified crimes I needed to make up for.

Years later I found out that the jolly, bearded figure cuddling all the young children on his lap *was* Grandad. He was man the locals trusted most to be close to their kids. My terrifying intuition had been right.

Afterwards, I watched Grandad walk round the stalls, greeting people loudly, with parents gathering round to have a chat with him. Everyone was congratulating him about the amount of money he'd raised for a local children's charity over the last few weeks. He brushed off their compliments politely, as if he was too humble to accept glory for it. I overheard him tell someone that 'the welfare of the children', was all that mattered. They squeezed his arm, smiled and replied what a good man he was, and how lucky we all were to have him around. As an adult, these memories make me choke with disbelief, but as a child they highlighted the fact that everyone loved Grandad, so in some way I must be the one in the wrong, who deserved what I got.

'You ready to get off home, little princess?' asked

Grandad, finally spying me playing with dolls behind the knitwear stall.

I nodded, fidgeting with the hem of my dress. Then I skipped over as he held his hand out to me. With other people around, we both fell into the pretence of normality, of how things were between us before the abuse started.

Driving home, Grandad turned the radio up loud and we sung along to all the Christmas hits. He was genuinely like Jekyll and Hyde. On days like this, it was hard to believe the reality of what he was doing to me in secret.

The house was warmer than usual when we arrived. Gran had put the heating up to stave off the cold winter chills. Tinsel was strung up on the walls, and greetings cards were crammed onto every available shelf.

'Brian's coming over later to pick up the presents for the kids,' said Gran, talking about my dad, as she rushed to get ready for work.

Dad also worked most weekends, and as Joan was often reluctant to look after me, Grandad had cunningly volunteered. Tom and my stepbrothers were all in their mid teens now and met up with friends on a Saturday night. There was no way Joan was going to stay in just to look after me, so most weekends were spent at Grandad's, with him babysitting me alone.

For once, Grandad didn't pounce on me as soon as she left. It's because Dad's coming round, I thought to myself, pleased at the reprieve.

Later that night, after my father had popped by, Grandad poured me a measure of alcohol. 'Here's a wee nip of whisky,' he said, winking.

He often tried to make me drink, saying it was a sign I was a 'big girl'. A swig of whisky always made me splutter with shock. It tasted foul.

Tonight, Grandad pointed out that everyone had a bit to drink at Christmas. I was only nine years old, but that didn't matter to him.

It was almost time for me to go to bed. Usually my ordeal would be over by now, and I felt so relieved that I'd somehow managed to escape it.

After reluctantly finishing my drink, I headed upstairs. I felt woozy, sleepy and happier than I had been in a long time. Had Grandad tired of our games? I prayed that he had. Or maybe he was just being kind because it was Christmas. Either way, I felt this was a positive turning point. If he left me alone once, it meant I could see an end to it.

Within minutes I drifted off into a deep, dreamy sleep.

At around midnight I woke up with that horrible, chilling feeling that someone's watching you. I opened my eyes sharply, and looked at the side of the bed. Nobody was there. I was alone in the room. Then I slowly raised my gaze towards the door, scared of what I would find. Above the door was a rectangular glass pane – and a shocking sight.

Through the darkness I could make out Grandad's piercing eyes staring in at me. He looked like a terrifying, disembodied head hovering above the outside of the door. I clutched my sheets in fear. What was he doing, watching me from the darkness of the corridor in the middle of the night?

Even though he was tall, I realized that he must be standing on something to be able to see through the window. The deliberateness of it frightened me even more. For a few minutes he remained in position, and I cowered under his intimidating gaze, wondering what I should do – and what he would do.

Then without a word he walked in and stood over the bed.

In the last few months he'd taken to lying on top of me in bed, and pushing against me. I kept my nightie on, but I could feel the change in him through the flimsy material. I know now he was simulating sex. But at the time, I felt he was crushing me to death. He was a big man, almost twice my size. When he was on top of me, I felt my ribs compress and I would gasp for breath, terrified he would kill me by mistake. If I cried out or told him to stop, he would put his hand over my mouth to shut me up. I'd wriggle away to lessen the pain, but he'd hold me down with even more force, almost breaking my arms with the pressure. Afterwards he'd tell me that it was my fault his 'lollipop' changed shape during these encounters. I'd feel humiliated and ashamed by this information. How could *I* have done that? I didn't want to do anything.

There was another worry in my mind too, and this *really* terrified me. I knew from painful experience that he liked to put objects in my 'flower', and that this hurt me more than anything. What if he tried to put his lollipop there? The thought played over and over in my mind with chilling repetition.

Tonight, he ordered me to remove my nightdress. I

tried to snuggle under the sheets, but he ripped them back, saying I should remove my pants too.

I shook my head, so he grabbed my arm and pulled them off angrily.

He pushed me down on the bed and climbed on top of me. Like before, he started pushing on top of me. But this time it was different. A rip of cold, searing pain rushed through my body. I cried out with a terrified sob, pleading for him to stop.

'Shut up,' he hissed. 'It'll only be sore for a bit.'

Grandad had told me about a little bit of skin I had in my flower. He said that when I was finally a big girl it was his job to remove it. That time had come, in the most horrific way. I struggled beneath him, feeling faint with the intensity of the pain.

'It only hurts because I'm removing the skin. It's perfectly normal,' he told me, trying to calm me down. He often talked about our games and my body in medical terms. Because he was a paramedic, and I was only a child, he manipulated my lack of knowledge and inherent respect for his opinions.

I could feel myself switch into pure panic mode. He was raping me. This felt more invasive and disgusting than anything he'd inflicted on me before. I thought he would kill me; that I would die of serious injuries. Then he suddenly stopped, collapsing on top of me, out of breath.

My pony-pattern duvet lay crumpled in a heap on the floor. The dark of the night was silent other than Grandad's rasping breath and the steady, deep heartbeat of my anguished sobs. I was in total, utter shock.

'Get yourself cleaned up,' he said brusquely, finally pulling himself together. He switched the light on, and gestured towards the bathroom.

I inched myself off the bed, feeling numb from the pain. As I sat on the edge of the bed and looked behind me I almost passed out. He'd made me lie on my white dressing gown. Now, the white fabric, kept pristinely clean by Gran, was soaked in angry red blood, absorbing into the fibres of the cotton and spreading slowly outwards. It looked like something from a murder scene. I'm dying, I thought to myself, *I'm dying*. My sobs turned into chokes and I gripped the bed tightly in a paralysing fear.

Grandad followed my look, and for a moment we were both transfixed by the physical evidence of what happens when you violate a nine-year-old.

'You're fine,' he said in a firm voice. 'It's okay, it's just a cut.'

I didn't answer. My breath was coming quick and fast. I was hyperventilating.

'Go to the bathroom and clean yourself up!' he shouted in my face.

The powerful force of his voice snapped me out of my shock. I stood up and limped towards the bathroom, holding my flower in my hands. I honestly thought my insides would fall out as soon as I stood up. It was the longest walk of my life. The pain and fear were unimaginable. Inside the bathroom, I steadied myself, leaning against the wall. I could hear a tap running as Grandad cleaned himself up in the downstairs toilet.

Looking in the mirror, I hardly recognized the small, frightened face looking back at me. My expression was that of a hunted animal who has tasted the blood of its own death in its mouth. My pupils were dilated so far my eyes appeared to have been swallowed whole by blackness. My skin was sheet white, and my lips were cracked with blood where I had bitten them in pain. The blood trickled down the insides of my legs and formed a pool on the floor, running into the grouting of the floor tiles.

I couldn't cry. I tried, but no tears came.

My physical wounds were bad, but that wasn't the worst of what he had done to me. As my immediate fear subsided, it was replaced by something that crawled through my soul, gnawing at my insides with disgust, shame and a feeling of hollowness. My first reaction had been that I was dying. Now I felt dead. In a way, Grandad had killed me. He had murdered something inside me, and the light that illuminates all children was switched off.

On the side of the bath was a metal scouring pad used to scrub the bath.

I crawled over and sat on the edge of the bath, trying to stem the flow of blood with toilet paper stuffed underneath my flower. Then I seized the metal scourer and started to scrub my skin, violently attacking the insides of my legs, my stomach and the flat area where my breasts would grow when I hit puberty. Scrubbing viciously, the tears finally came. They were hysterical, rage-fuelled sobs from the belly as I tore away at my skin.

Please make me feel clean again, I begged. I felt so dirty.

But no amount of water or scrubbing could remove the indelible mark he had left on me – although God knows I tried.

That was the start of my self-harming, trying to scrub away his evil touch.

I felt I would never be clean again.

8. Twisted Tales

After the rape was the first time I seriously considered telling my secret.

Something had snapped inside me, and Grandad's previous threats paled into the background under the shadow of this new fear and pain.

But it was as though he was psychic.

The next morning I woke up in agony. The night before, adrenalin and alcohol had helped numb me a little, but now the pain crippled me. It was Monday morning and I was due at school. Grandad greeted me in the morning with a cup of tea and a bowl of cereal.

'Breakfast in bed,' he said cheerily, as though nothing out of the ordinary had happened.

He was speaking in a loud voice so Gran could hear. Then he sat on the bed, and in a lower tone whispered, 'If you want to tell your dad what's happened, I'll call him for you now.' His manner was nonchalant.

This stunned me. It was the last thing I expected him to say.

'Of course, if I tell him ...' there was a loaded pause, 'I'll also have to say how bad you've been.' He pondered, looking intently at me. 'He'll probably have to send you away.' It was pure reverse psychology.

My mind raced with possibilities. But it finally arrived

at the overriding fear of being abandoned, left alone with no one to love me.

If Grandad could do this to me, what was to say other people wouldn't?

In a children's home things could be much worse.

I'd just have to stay silent. So I shook my head meekly, saying there was no need to tell Dad.

During the drive to school I'd never seen Grandad so elated – and evil. He knew he'd got me. If I didn't tell after rape, he could do what he liked. Brimming with confidence he talked non-stop about sex during the whole journey. He told me he'd done this to other little girls, and claimed that they liked it. I sat in silence, trying to breathe deeply and ignore the throbbing pain. For me, this was as bad as it could get – but apparently there was worse ahead.

Grandad started talking about things I hadn't done yet, sexual things he'd tried with other little girls. He implied they enjoyed it and that they were better at it than me. Unbelievably he was playing on childish insecurities to try and make me accept what he was doing, and work harder to please him.

'You're not as good as other little girls at it,' he told me. 'They were so good they got to go back to their mummys. That's what you need to do.'

He dropped me off outside the school gates and handed me a note. It excused me from gym saying I'd stayed over and forgotten my PE kit.

My whole body was red raw, and I felt ashamed and embarrassed.

Kids were racing round the playground, full of high

spirits as I shuffled along, wracked with pain. No one noticed anything was wrong with me.

I was a nerd, a geek, a teacher's pet – the kind of person the cool crowd ignored. A few of the older girls had started casually bullying me, but nothing serious yet. Just name calling and undisguised contempt.

At lunchtime I hid under the stairs in the assembly hall. Anybody walking up them wouldn't have a clue I was there. Huddled alone, I sniffled tears and felt more desolate than ever. I wanted more than anything to tell Dad what was happening, but I knew I couldn't. I was trapped in this nightmare, scared of what was next.

Arriving home that night, I was quiet and withdrawn. Joan didn't notice or she didn't care. Instead she was waiting for me in the living room almost shaking with fury. Staying overnight at Grandad's, I'd left my book behind in my bedroom. In my absence, Joan had decided to have a snoop round. Picking it up off my bedside table the bookmark must have fallen out.

'What's THIS??' she shrieked at me, waving a photo in my face.

It was an old battered picture of my mum and dad together. The sides were curled up and the colour faded, but you could still see their happy smiles as they held hands all those years ago. I used it as a bookmark to remind me of happier times. It was an anchor in this sea of chaos.

'Are you doing this to spite me?' she screamed, little spots of spit flying out of her mouth as she shook me, fast losing control of her vicious temper.

I don't know why she was so insecure about her new marriage to feel this way. As she carried on ranting I looked at her in bemusement.

Finally her rage was spent, and luckily she didn't thrash me with the belt. But it was the final straw to the worst few days of my life so far.

I trudged upstairs and climbed into bed with Lassie. Her fur was soft against my tender skin, and for the first time I felt slightly comforted.

'I don't like these games. Should I tell Dad?' I asked her earnestly.

She woofed, and I took that as a no. Lassie didn't want me to be sent away either. Whatever happened, at least we had each other.

By my twelfth birthday I was mature enough to pick up on all the severity of the tensions in the house. I couldn't understand why, but I sensed that something was brewing. Everything was falling apart at home. Joan and I were at each other's throats all the time – or rather she was at mine. The more horrific Grandad's abuse became, the more erratic my behaviour got.

I wasn't a trouble-maker; I was *odd*. At times painfully shy, others bizarrely attention-seeking. My lies got bigger and bolder, and my jaunts off to the peace of the cemetery and the woods became more frequent. Maybe a mother would have spotted that something was seriously wrong. But Joan wasn't my mum. She didn't care a jot about me.

To make matters worse, for some reason Dad believed every word that came out of her mouth. Looking back he must have been having a hard time in a tough new job.

Put that alongside a painful divorce, losing one child when he left with his mum to go to England, then gaining two stepsons, it must have been a real emotional struggle. A dysfunctional daughter was probably the final straw. No wonder he left raising the kids to Joan.

But that was no help to me. Joan's and my mutual hatred got bigger and bigger – until finally it threatened to blow the family apart.

The day the storm broke, I'd decided to take Lassie for a walk in the woods. We were heading home, walking back through the village, muddy grass stuck to our respective paws and shoes. The nights were getting lighter, and the countryside had that fresh feel of something preparing to come into bloom. Looking closely, I could see new shoots on the trees and the odd daffodil poking its pretty head up in shady woodlands. Getting away from everything and being alone with nature always recharged me, and I was feeling quite jaunty as we trotted along together.

From behind me I heard a car and instinctively looked back. It was a police car. My dad was behind the wheel and I waved happily in his direction. But when he drove closer I could see a worried frown on his face as he signalled for me to head straight back home.

Here we go, I thought. I'm in trouble again. What is it now?

Joan loved to call Dad when he was at work and stress him out by complaining about me and telling him my latest tall stories. I resigned myself to always being the one to blame for everything.

As I arrived home, intuition told me this was different.

The living-room door was closed and Lassie, full of high sprits, burst through it paws first, barking with glee.

Dad was pacing round the living room and Joan looked smug.

My first thought was, Have they found out? But I instantly dismissed this.

'Go upstairs,' said Dad.

I couldn't work out his mood. I carefully took Lassie off the lead, and headed for my bedroom. Dad followed me up and sat next to me on the bed.

'You know I love you, don't you?'

I mumbled yes, terrified as to where this conversation was going.

He hesitated, and a tortured look crossed his face. 'But Joan just can't cope with you any more, especially with me at work all the time.'

I still didn't get what he meant, and looked at him in bewilderment.

'We've decided you should go and live with your grandad for a while – just to give you and Joan some space to calm things down.'

If he'd detonated a nuclear bomb I couldn't have been more distraught.

'Please no, I'll change, I'll do anything,' I begged him, tears flooding down my face. I lost the plot and began clawing at his trousers, throwing myself on him, begging repeatedly for him to change his mind. I nearly screamed everything out. He was sending me into the lion's den. It was like handing me over to the devil himself.

Dad leaned forward to give me a big hug. He thought

I was crying because I didn't want to leave my home, and because it sounded like he preferred Joan.

'Don't worry, Gran and Grandad love you,' he said, trying to console me. 'We can still see each other at weekends.'

With the mention of Grandad my sobbing became hysterical.

'Please no. I'll behave, I'll go straight to my room from school and never speak to anyone, it'll be as though I'm not here,' I promised him.

But it had already been decided. No doubt, Grandad had played a big part in that decision, suggesting the perfect solution to everyone's problem.

How convenient for him.

I started to fall apart at this news. It was as if the black chasm hanging over my life had just swallowed me whole. I was shaking so hard I thought I was going to have a fit. I couldn't stop the trembling in my stomach, and it threatened to take over my body. I felt so angry that this was a done deal and I had no say in it. Once again, I was totally at the mercy of the adults who surrounded me.

I was too scared to tell anyone what was happening, but part of me wished they would guess. Were they total idiots? I wondered to myself. Didn't they stop and think why I acted so weirdly or why I had no friends at school? I knew they had family debates about it, but in the past they had put it down to the divorce. That excuse was stretched thin, and they reasoned I should be over it by now. They were clueless as to what was really going on.

Of course, like me, they were also manipulated by Grandad. As the respected elder of the family, he would have presided over any discussions about me. If anyone got dangerously close to the truth or started asking awkward questions, he would cunningly steer them away to safer territory: like the divorce. He would reassure them it was just a stage I was going through. He'd probably persuaded them it was better if I stayed with him until things had blown over and I'd grown up a little bit. For Dad, it must have seemed a life raft to save him from the escalating turmoil in our family. He probably thought I loved Grandad, who treated me like a princess in public, and that I would only be living ten minutes' drive away.

But he didn't know the truth. He had no idea that Grandad was raping and sexually torturing me, tormenting me with lies about being unloved.

After my hysterical outburst at the news, Dad finally realized that nothing he could say would comfort or calm me down. So giving me one last hug, he headed down stairs. The first person he called was Grandad.

'We've told her and she's really upset . . .' I overheard him say.

Then silence as Grandad spoke.

'No she doesn't want to go,' he explained, his voice trembling.

Again, silence as Grandad replied at the other end of the line.

'Okay, I'll see you in a bit . . . thanks.'

I guessed correctly that Grandad was heading straight over.

He didn't want his master plan to be ruined by me. It was like watching a pantomime with no audience to shout 'he's behind you' when the villain appears. Dad thought he was doing the right thing, but he was falling into a trap carefully laid by his father, who wanted me as his permanent plaything.

I sat on my bed in stunned silence. Tears were blurring my eyes, making the wallpaper appear even more psychedelic than usual. In the corner of the room was an expensive karaoke machine. Dad had gone mad when Grandad had given it to me as a present, saying he spoiled me too much. 'She's my special little girl,' he'd replied, shrugging his shoulders.

I heard the front door click. He was here already. I could hear the murmurs of hushed conversation downstairs, and every so often I managed to pick out my grandfather's reassuring words. Then the sound of his boots reverberated on the staircase.

'Don't be so silly,' he said, towering above me. 'You'll be sent to a home if you carry on like this – or your dad will lock you up in the police cell.'

His tone was stern and annoyed. Downstairs, they probably thought he was soothing me with kind words. Instead, he was trying to intimidate me.

'It's just like I told you – everyone gets fed up with you. First your mum didn't want you, now your dad doesn't want you. I'm the only person you've got. I'm the only one who can put up with you.' He pressed his face close to mine, and almost snarled.

What he said was awful beyond measure, but it made sense. Mum *had* left me, Dad *didn't* want me. Grandad wasn't making this up, it was all true – it had actually happened. Maybe he was the only person I could trust. He told me that lots of other little children played games with him. Maybe it was normal? Or at least the only way for a lonely little girl to survive . . .

My sobs reduced to a sad sniffle.

'That's better,' he said consolingly, speaking more gently now.

Once again, my mind fractured into a split personality. I reasoned that if I could somehow keep in Grandad's good books – and Dad's – then one day the abuse might stop, and I'd still be part of a family. That was all that mattered.

I walked downstairs holding his hand, and I could see the look of relief in my dad's eyes. Once again, to everyone else Grandad was the hero.

It was decided that I should move in with my grandparents at the end of the summer holidays, before I went to secondary school, closer to their house.

As she was the family dog, I would have to leave Lassie. The thought choked me up so much I could barely think of it. To make up for it, I was bought a Shetland pony that was kept at the nearby farm of a family friend. Grandad would take me up there on trips, and I'd groom my new horse, growing to love my new friend.

But not all our little trips were so innocent. Mostly, they were painful, humiliating tours through the worst kind of sexual terror.

Grandad had taken to parking near a well-known beauty spot while he abused me. Incredibly, the allure wasn't that it was secluded but that a busy road was nearby. He had become so sure of himself, he was getting off on the exhibitionism of what he could do to me, with no one finding out. He'd park, and for a few moments we'd sit in silence admiring the view. Of course, I wouldn't be admiring anything. My eyes would be almost blind with the fear of what he was about to do to me. Usually he'd linger over a cigarette, the smoke smothering me as I sat obediently by his side.

Opening the door to stub it out was the sign my ordeal was about to begin.

He'd touch me roughly, pushing me onto my knees, the gravel stabbing into my skin as I was forced to perform oral sex on him. The angle of the open car door obscured me from view, and to drivers passing by he just looked like an old man taking in the scenery. Sometimes he'd get so carried away, he'd force me round the back of the car, push me across the boot and rape me as the cars whizzed by in a rainbow blur.

The exposure frightened me more, just as it increased his excitement.

Afterwards, I'd go home and slip back into the role of being a normal twelve-year-old girl. It was something I had to fake. I had no clue what normal was any more. I'd watch the girls at school flirt with boys, starting to develop the very first buds of a precocious pre-pubescent sexual awareness. I couldn't relate to them. I wasn't interested in boys, I just wanted to be left alone.

The only high point of these last couple of months living at the police station – on remand as I saw it – was an exciting school assignment. Each student had to pick a topic to write a project on. There was no contest for me: my favourite subject in the world was witchcraft and local folklore.

I spent weeks doing research. I asked all the old locals for their memories of ancient folklore from the area, and holed myself up in the library looking through long-forgotten documents. When I eventually handed it in, I got top marks for my work. For the first time in ages, I felt really proud of myself.

I skipped home to show my dad how well I'd done, clutching my project with my childish handwriting scribbled on every page, along with drawings and even maps of the local area, relevant to witchcraft.

Bursting through the door, my exuberance was deflated by seeing Grandad sitting at the dining table, the whiff of his strong aftershave stinking out the room.

I paused for a moment before remembering my good news.

'I got top marks!' I said excitedly, unable to stop my boasting.

'That's fantastic,' said Dad, coming over to give me a congratulatory kiss. Joan ignored me, and flounced into the kitchen. Since the decision that I was moving, we had barely spoken to each other. But at least she didn't use the belt on me as much.

Dad was in a rush to get back to his shift, so he didn't have time to look at the project, even though he was really pleased I'd done well.

'Are you going to show me what you've done?' asked Grandad, standing up and walking over. He knelt down on one knee and started to flick through the pages, looking impressed by what he saw. I couldn't help but beam.

'Grandad's taking you over to his,' said Joan in a surly

manner, ignoring the praise being heaped upon me. As always, if I shone, she felt insecure.

It's hard to explain how I felt on hearing this news. Even though deep in my heart I knew what this meant for me, I still managed to separate it from that precise moment, otherwise I would have gone insane. I could detach myself completely from the future and from the present when I was being abused. I learnt to snatch simple pleasures happening in the moment. At this minute, I'd done well at school, Grandad and Dad were both pleased with me, and I wasn't in pain or upset. That's all I focused on. I didn't dwell on what might be happening in an hour or a few days' time. I couldn't live that way.

Grandad seemed to be genuinely interested in my project, asking me lots of questions about what I'd found out – and how I'd done it.

I explained that in 1563 a Witchcraft Act had been passed. That meant lots of witch hunts in Scotland, where the witches were often tortured into confessing their guilt. Often they were dropped in water; if they survived it was another sign of guilt. Then they were either burned at the stake or hung.

Grandad nodded his head with interest, telling me to carry on.

I told him that there was a witchcraft panic in the sixteenth century when witches were accused of treason against King James VI. But in 1736 the Witchcraft Act was repealed.

'What about local witches?' asked Grandad curiously, after my lecture.

'Well, let me show you this map,' I replied, surprised but glad he'd asked the question.

Near the outskirts of the village, on the riverbank, was a spot famous for the persecution of witches. I'd even drawn a map showing exactly how to get there.

'I tell you what, why don't we drive there now?' he said enthusiastically.

In my childish way I was really pleased he was taking such an interest in my work. It never occurred to me he had a sinister agenda.

The drive only took a few minutes. It was a blustery day with bright skies and occasional bursts of sunshine. I led him down to a rocky crag, jutting into the murky river. Holding the map in my hand, I scrambled down the bank and followed a narrow muddy footpath winding round the rocks. Grandad climbed down after me, grunting with the effort. Finally, we jumped onto a little sandy beach, with small waves lapping around our feet. It was completely secluded and even though you could hear passing traffic, it was completely out of sight.

Grandad was out of breath, but I was full of energy and excitement.

'Here it! Here it is!' I cried out, eagerly pointing to a large jagged rock that loomed over the little sheltered cove.

'What is it?' he asked, looking curiously up at the rock.

'In the old days, witches used to be imprisoned here as the tide was rising to see if they were guilty!' I explained triumphantly.

I couldn't believe Grandad was paying me this much attention, and I carried on speaking rapidly, telling him all about the history I had learned.

Above us, welded into the imposing rock, was an iron neck brace, rusted by the tides and rain, but still as strong as ever. In medieval times, women would be forced against the rock, with the wrought-iron collar snapped shut across their necks, then bolted in place. The waters would rise as their hopeless cries drifted across the shores. It was a terrifying mechanism, which looked like the pictures of torture instruments I'd seen in books on the London Dungeon. I couldn't help but shudder as we got closer to it. It looked so out of place against the backdrop of the peaceful sounds of running water and winds whistling through gaps in the rocks. Even though it was just a strip of metal, it had an evil presence, which you felt the nearer you got.

'Let's have a proper look at it,' said Grandad, pulling himself up onto the slate ledge under the rock – where all those helpless women would have stood in the past. I'd never seen him look so animated or intrigued.

I followed closely at his heels, tugging at his trousers for leverage.

Within seconds we were standing on the ledge together.

Maybe I should have suspected something, or at least felt uneasy, but I didn't. It's amazing how resilient childhood innocence is – I never suspected for a second what he was about to do.

'Why don't you stand against the rock to see how it works?' he asked.

It sounded like a good idea, as if it was another part of my school project.

I was too small for my neck to reach the iron collar, so Grandad hoisted me up and told me to wedge my feet against a small ledge in the rock to support myself. It was quite precarious and my heart started beating faster.

'That's right.' Grandad reassured me, moving my neck up to the collar.

Finally, I was in place. Suddenly he slammed it shut. My head jammed painfully into the rough surface of the rock and the iron pressed into my neck making my feel strangled. I automatically clawed to pull it away, but Grandad pushed my hands off and held it firmly in place, trapping me. I went to scream out, but then I caught a glimpse of the expression on his face. It was one of pure malevolence. The mixture of glee and sadism in his eyes made me wince with fear. He didn't even look like the same man he had been only moments ago. It was as though he had stumbled onto his own private torture chamber and once again, I was to be his victim. He hadn't been interested in my project. He had only wanted to get me here to indulge in his sick fantasies. I was terrified.

'Please don't,' I begged, knowing it was pointless.

'Shut up!' he hissed, removing my pants with his free hand.

Even though it was summer, there was a sharp sea breeze and I was cold and frightened. I imagined that the gulls circling overhead were crying out for help on my behalf. But once again, I was alone and at his mercy.

Seeing me trapped, shivering like a frightened animal in a snare, evidently turned Grandad on. He enjoyed seeing me struggle against my metal shackle, my little legs kicking out furiously as he started to abuse me.

His violent touch instantly reduced me to panicked sobs. But try as I might to escape, the neck brace held me firmly in place. I was utterly helpless. For some reason, this felt infinitely scarier than my usual ordeals. Maybe it was knowing that other women, including many accused witches, had suffered in the same spot. My vivid imagination made me feel even more powerless and small knowing what had happened in this place.

Afterwards, Grandad left me hanging limp in the collar while he made his way down to the shore, looking back as if he wanted to frame this image in his mind for ever. I wish I were dead, I thought to myself in shock.

After my stifled screams and Grandad's muffled threats, there was silence. I looked across the bay, squinting through my tears. Nothing but trees, birds and water. There was no one to witness my pain. The whisper of the water, which had been soothing before, now seemed sinister.

I prised the collar open, my little hands pushing hard against the iron.

The blood trickled down my legs, snaking its way to my white ankle socks. Soaked crimson, they could be thrown away. But the suffering imprinted on my soul would be harder to erase.

Being a local man, Grandad had obviously known the landmark. He'd played on my innocence so that I would take him there, and walk into his trap. His evil knew no limits.

9. In His Clutches

'Raggy doll! Scabby queen!' a couple of girls taunted me as I walked across the playground with my head bowed. I was twelve years old and it was my first day at big school. The bullies from my last school had grouped together and formed a clique, and I was an easy target. They sensed my vulnerability – it was as if my jugular had been left wide open for them. Joan didn't bother about how I looked. At first she'd tried to keep up appearances, but eventually she stopped bothering. If anyone asked, she blamed me, saying I was scruffy by nature. So I went to school with buttons missing from my shirt, my hair tangled and uncombed, generally looking dishevelled. It was evident no one really cared about me so the bullies teased me mercilessly, calling me names.

This was my first day having escaped the clutches of Joan – only to be delivered into the arms of what I saw to be the devil himself: Grandad. The plan was that after my first day at my new school, rather than returning home, he'd pick me up to start my new life with him and Gran.

So today was a triple whammy. Not only did I leave the home, father and dog I loved, I started at a scary new school I hated, where bullies picked on me and, to top it all, I then moved in with an evil monster who was sexually abusing me, with an escalating degree of violence.

My life felt like a nightmare, within a nightmare.

The last few weeks had been hell. After the shock of the initial decision, I'd managed to put it out of my mind. With months to go until the move, I tried not think about the horror I would face. But when it got perilously close, I started to freak out. Badly.

I began to beg Dad again, pleading day after day for him to reconsider his decision. There were times when I could tell he was wavering, but if he ever had doubts, Joan would be there to strengthen his resolve. Grandad piled on the pressure too. Dad obviously discussed my distress with him, asking for his advice. I'd hear them in the living room in big family meetings chatting about it earnestly.

'She's really upset,' I'd hear Dad say, a quaver in his voice.

'Och, she'll get used to it. In a few weeks she'll be skipping round happily – all kids get scared by change. They don't know what's best for them,' Grandad would argue back in his most persuasive tone.

Joan would back him up. 'We can't continue like this – it's her or me. This is best for everyone.'

Dad didn't want me to go to Yorkshire to stay with Mum, because he'd hardly ever get to see me. He told himself this was only a temporary measure to calm things down between me and Joan, and convinced himself that it wasn't even worth mentioning to Mum. He wasn't the one who wanted me to move, it was everyone else who was applying the pressure.

I'd hear Dad sigh with resignation, saying, 'I suppose you're right.'

I'd stifle the sobs in my pillow and imagine running down the stairs and screaming, 'Do you know what he's doing to me?!'

So many times during those last weeks I was a hair's breadth away from telling him. But whenever I got close, Grandad or Joan would miraculously pop up. Sensing there was a danger Dad would change his mind, Grandad visited the house constantly during those last few weeks. Just in case.

By now my absolute fear over what Grandad was doing to me was so intense I wasn't as worried about being sent away. What could be worse than this? I thought to myself. With Joan's punishments I'd learned that there were different kinds of horrors to those of sexual abuse. If my life got worse, at least it would be a different kind of misery. And at this moment, anything seemed better than what was actually happening. I'd rather be starved or beaten than endure what Grandad was doing to me. The problem was, I couldn't find the words to say what was happening. I'd try to think how to blurt it out, and my mind would go blank.

But if someone had pressed the right triggers, I would have broken down and confessed everything.

'I don't want to go and live with Grandad,' I would say. 'He's an old man who doesn't like little girls.' My emphasis was always on the fact I didn't want to live with *Grandad* – not that I didn't want to move. But no one picked up on it. If someone had asked the right question, and enquired what was wrong with Grandad, it would have come tumbling out. But no one would have guessed in a million years he was the problem.

Over the last few years I'd built a brick wall round myself, now I felt it was starting to crumble. I'd never felt so desperate in my life. I even resorted to begging Joan to let me stay. I was almost on my knees, promising her things, saying I'd call her mum, telling her I'd love her more.

She just looked at me with contempt and said, 'We need the break.'

I tried one last time with Dad. 'I'll be good,' I sobbed. But nothing worked.

So I decided it was easier to put the brick wall back up again. I knew Grandad would carry on raping, abusing and torturing me, but I figured my only hope was escape. My life for the present was wrecked – all I could do was pray that at some point it would get better. It had to. It really did.

In retrospect, if Dad felt he couldn't cope with me any more, I should really have been sent to live with my mum. But Grandad made sure that didn't happen. Mum wasn't even told until it was a done deal. As it was never framed as a permanent move, it wasn't considered a big issue.

I still spoke to my mum on the phone every few weeks, but I was a little girl and we didn't have intimate con-versations. She'd ask about school, tell me she loved me, then ring off. I was never told *not* to mention the move, but it was planted in my head that it would be better not to bother her with something so trivial. I didn't want to cause trouble, so I kept quiet.

After I resigned myself to leaving I asked my dad one last favour.

'Can I take Lassie with me?' I pleaded, tears streaming down my face.

She was my soulmate and the best and only friend I'd ever had. It sounds silly now, but I was more upset about leaving that dog than my family.

But the answer was no. Dad said she was settled at the police station, and that it wouldn't be fair to Gran to have a big, boisterous dog in the house.

Leaving Lassie broke my heart into pieces. It took the last bit of hope and solace I had away from me. It really, really tore me apart.

'I love you so much,' I whispered, nuzzling into her grass-scented fur, soaking it with tears. The night before I left, I crept down to the living room after everyone was asleep and smuggled her into my bedroom so she could sleep with me. I cuddled up to her and had a proper conversation, explaining that I was leaving, and she mustn't be upset.

'I'm going away, but you're not to worry,' I told her, trying to choke back the sobs. 'I promise I'll be okay. I'll come back at the weekends and tell you all my secrets still.' I felt that I had to put on a brave face for my little dog. But I don't know who I was trying to reassure, Lassie or me. She did a low little woof and licked my nose. Somehow, I felt she understood. Maybe I just needed to think that some living creature cared.

As with my mum, I can't actually remember saying goodbye to Dad. Maybe I just blocked it out. I left for school that day knowing I wouldn't return.

School was hell. I'd found it hard to fit into a tiny village school, but a large, unruly comprehensive was truly intimidating. I stood on my own at lunchtime, wondering if I would always lose everything I loved. But much as I longed for the final bell to ring, I also feared it. It meant it was time to go home – to my new torture chamber.

Grandad picked me up looking like a man who had won the lottery.

Over the last few weeks my belongings had been gradually moved out of the police station. On my last night there, it was like sleeping in an empty shell. The hollowness of what had been my safe little nest was symbolic.

My new bedroom – the spare room I usually slept in at Grandad's, the same one I was also ritually raped, battered and abused in – had been redecorated to mark my arrival as a full-time resident of the house.

All those years back, when Grandad began grooming me, he had manipulated me with money, buying treats and pampering me. In the long years since then, such niceties had ended. I hated him. I hated what he was doing to me, and he didn't disguise the fact that he didn't care about me, other than what he could do to my body. He'd long since abandoned winning me over with bribes and nice behaviour. Other people might not have paid enough attention to notice it, but being on the receiving end, I did.

That all changed now. My moving in must have been the fulfilment of a long-cherished ambition for him but he realized that I could spoil it all for him, so he set about trying to 'win me over'. Doing up my room was just the start of his campaign.

In the car, he looked at me and grinned, revealing his nicotine-stained yellow teeth. 'We've got your room done. You're going to love your grandad when you see it,' he told me.

By this point, I never reacted to anything with a single emotion. The two sides of my split personality had their own individual responses. The innocent, childish side of me was excited, screaming, 'Yay! What colour's the wallpaper? Is my favourite rag doll there?' But the other side of me, the abused girl who knew too much, screamed, 'I'm walking into hell here. There's a terrible price to pay for this.'

We went through the front door and the lock clicked. I felt like a trapped animal who had watched the cage door slowly lower down. Now it had locked shut.

Gran was in the kitchen and shouted out, 'Ten minutes until dinner.' She was an unsentimental old lady, and didn't make a fuss over my moving in.

Despite the smells of cooking sausage, mash and peas drifting through the house, the walls seemed to be closing in on me. This is my home now, I thought.

'There's a special surprise in your room,' said Grandad, looking pleased with himself. I ran up the stairs to see what it was.

My room looked lovely. The wallpaper was multi-coloured rainbows and stars, and on the ceiling were stars that glowed in the dark. It was magical. Resting on top of the bed was a brand new Barbie, with a shiny blue Beetle car by her side. I squealed with joy. I was still a girly girl.

I didn't notice the new wardrobe at first. It was white, with two doors separated by a full-length mirror. The reflection was a perfectly complete view of the bed, like a television screen of whatever you happened to be doing on there. No doubt, Grandad had chosen it on purpose.

He was doing everything in his power to make the move happy for me, so I wouldn't kick up a fuss and threaten his plan. You'd have thought he'd ease up on the abuse for a while too, but not a chance. He was like a man with a sweet tooth in a sweet shop. He couldn't control himself.

Since the abuse began, Grandad had always used the excuse that I was 'growing up', saying this was what 'big girls' did. Every birthday was a reason for him to step up his attacks on me. Within a week of my moving in, he had an even better excuse.

One morning I woke up to find my new bed sheets stained bright red. My first reaction was panic. Was I dying? Had the abuse damaged me?

I ran to my grandfather. Ironically, because he was a paramedic, he was the first person I thought of to save me. He rushed in – then grinned.

'You've got your period,' he stated simply. Then he shouted for Gran to break the news to her. She hugged me saying, 'You're not a wee girl now.'

'Yes, you're all grown up,' added Grandad, with knowing menace.

Gran didn't pick up on any dark undertones, she was genuinely proud.

Moments later I sat shivering downstairs with a cup of tea, cringing as I heard Gran telephoning all my female relatives to break the news.

That kind of thing was a big deal in our family.

Mum was thrilled, telling me, 'Congratulations, you're a woman now!'

Without knowing it, they were reinforcing everything Grandad said.

I was a proper grown-up now and a few days later, I found out *exactly* what being classed as an adult meant.

Grandad had lavished money on me during my first two weeks at the house. Suddenly, he changed tactics.

'You know you're quite selfish,' he said to me one day as I sat playing in the living room. I looked at him, shocked. 'I've spent all that money on you, and you haven't bought anything for me,' he continued. He knew I didn't have any money, other than a few pounds spending money. I was confused and hurt by what he said. Was I being bad again? I worried.

'Look, I tell you what. I'll give you the money to buy a present for me – from you,' he suggested. It sounded like a good idea, and I nodded happily.

We set off in the car for the shops. As we headed into town he mentioned again that getting my period meant I was a finally a woman.

'It's time to wear big girls' clothes now,' he advised me. 'You can't wear those pants and vests for ever.'

I didn't know what he meant. I'd never really thought about adult underwear. Pants were just pants as far as I was concerned.

He pulled up outside a department store and ordered me to go inside and buy a suspender belt, stockings and a basque.

'Tell them it's a present for your auntie if anyone asks,'

he warned me. Obviously it would be odd to the assistants seeing a little girl, wandering round alone, buying sexy underwear.

'Oh and say she's about your size,' he added, stuffing a bunch of crumpled ten pounds notes into my hands. His palms were damp and sticky.

Walking around the shop I was totally lost. I had no idea what I was looking for. What were suspenders? I felt panicked. Eventually a kindly assistant came over and asked if I needed any help. I explained what I wanted and did exactly as Grandad had told me, saying it was for my auntie. The assistant looked puzzled when I said she was about the same size as me.

'She's very skinny,' I mumbled as a way of explanation.

Reassured, she held the basque and suspenders up against me. The contrast with my school uniform was uncomfortable in the extreme. Underwired bra cups jutted out, needing boobs to fill them. But I only had tiny buds.

As soon as I saw the underwear I knew what Grandad was planning. He often had me parading around in Gran's slips and high heels. This was the next step. I couldn't quite work out what this underwear was for, but I sensed it was something only for grown-ups – like something saucy your mum might wear, but you'd get in trouble for having.

Since I'd moved in, Grandad's entire attitude to me had changed. Perversely, he didn't treat me like a little girl he was abusing any more – he pretended I really was a woman. It was like he'd fallen for his own lies. He was still forceful and violent during the rapes, as I struggled and begged him to stop. But before the sexual abuse started, he treated me like I was his mistress. That sickened me more than anything.

As I slid back into the car, he snatched the carrier bag away from me eagerly.

'Did you get them?' He could barely contain the excitement in his voice.

I nodded and looked out of the window across the black tarmac road. I could see kids trotting behind their mums and old couples doddering along together. It was a world I no longer belonged to. My life had become gradually isolated from what the average person expected and enjoyed. It was like being in a prison where no one else could see the walls. Watching the world go by through the glass of the car window summed up my feeling of separation from any kind of normality. I was twelve years old and I had just bought suspenders and a basque for my grandad's enjoyment while he raped me. It was beyond twisted.

Back home, Grandad was even more fidgety than usual while Gran pottered around, preparing to go off to her job. She was the most-hard working woman I knew. It was a fine trait, but one that played to my disadvantage.

As soon as she left, he poured me a glass of whisky. I took a slow sip with a jaded air of acceptance. I didn't flinch any more as the liquid burned my throat. I was used to it. The only problem was the pain it caused in the cuts and sores from my oral rapes.

He rolled a slender cigarette, but rather than smoking it, he passed it to me. As I held it limply in my mouth, he lit it with a cheap yellow lighter from the local garage.

The smoke choked my lungs, and I tried not to inhale. Instead I puffed comically, looking uncomfortable. It was as if he imagined I was an adult woman embarking on a dangerous liaison with him. Sipping on my whisky, smoking a cigarette, I don't know what he saw – because I was a child and, for a normal person, it would have been a shocking sight. But in his sick mind he twisted it. I was 'all grown up'. Not that he liked the realities beyond his sick fantasies. Along with my periods, I had also started to develop pubic hair. He hated it. He wanted me to act grown up but still look like a little girl. To solve the problem, he'd bought me a packet of razors to shave down there. At first I refused, terrified by his request. Annoyed, he did it himself, cutting me in his angry impatience. After that, I agreed to do it myself. It disgusted me, but I had no choice.

Tonight, he made sure I was prepared for this new part of our 'games'.

'Why don't you go upstairs and try your new clothes on?' he suggested.

I hated the way he talked as if it was a new school uniform, or one of Gran's latest hand-knitted jumpers. He was trying to make it sound normal.

Walking upstairs, clutching the carrier bag, a wave of nausea came over me. He literally made me feel sick. In the weeks before I'd moved in, I'd thrown up nearly every day. Everyone thought I had a delicate stomach, but the reality was that I couldn't stand what Grandad was doing to me. By now my fear was buried deeper, becoming something darker. A normal person's first reaction to a frightening situation is to escape, but I knew that wasn't an option. When there's no way out, you have to swallow your fear and eventually it poisons you, sinking deep into every part of you. Every cell in my body was pulsing with a suppressed scream.

Standing in my bedroom, I pulled the basque on while staring blankly at the rainbow-patterned wallpaper. The dim light in the room meant the artificial stars were twinkling on the ceiling above my head. I caught a glimpse of myself in the mirror: I looked ridiculous. The basque was wearing me, not the other way round. Without fully developed boobs or womanly curves to hold it up, it just hung there in a sorry fashion. I picked up the suspender belt and looked at it with confusion. It was so complicated and fiddly I couldn't work out how to wear it. Why do women wear these things? I thought to myself. Why do men like them? It bewildered me. I was too young and physically undeveloped to realize that lingerie was meant to accentuate the shape of the female body. Being a child, it was beyond my grasp.

'What's taking you so long?' I could hear Grandad shouting up the stairs in exasperation, huffing as he climbed the steps. He'd wanted me to come down with a big showbiz-style surprise and parade around modelling for him, like he made me do with Gran's clothes. But it was too late for that.

I didn't need to explain what was wrong – he could see I was in a pickle.

'Here, let me do it,' he said, bending down to fix the stocking to the suspender belt. His breath stank as he came close to me.

Then, with no words or preamble, he pushed me onto the bed and raped me.

He was always rough and aggressive, but tonight he was worse than usual. It was as if the underwear had done something to him; he was like a savage animal. In his mind, wearing lingerie, I really was a woman. And not one he felt he had to treat nicely. I could tell he was perversely turned on as he pinned my wrists above my head, then used one hand to throttle me until I could barely breath. Still, he said nothing.

As usual I sobbed, cried and begged him to stop. Sometimes my crying would annoy him, other times it would turn him on, often it would send him into an angry rage. I kept on pleading. He kept ignoring me.

Afterwards I lay on the bed, the stockings ripped from their clasps, sobbing.

'I'm only showing you how to be a big girl,' he told me dismissively, as if he was doing me a favour and teaching me something important.

I rolled over so I didn't have to face him. My contempt for him was obvious. In public we still put on a pretence, both slipping on our masks, but in private he acted as though I was worthless, and I pushed my hatred as far as I could. But nothing seemed to touch a nerve with him. He was beyond human emotion. His cruelty was endless. When I'd overhear him telling neighbours he'd chosen to be a paramedic because he wanted to help people, I almost broke into hysterical laughter. To think that in the day he was racing around in an ambulance, trying to save lives, patching up injuries, cleaning away blood and trying to put people back together again. Then he'd come home and rip me apart until I was broken and bleeding. It's a contradiction that still shocks me.

The next day I woke up with mottled purple bruises on both my wrists from where he had pinned me down with such force. As always, he had a solution. Even though I usually wore short-sleeved shirts to school, he managed to dig out a long-sleeved one.

'Here's a note to get you out of gym class,' he told me calmly.

My life with him felt like one long premeditated murder.

He carefully stashed the underwear in one of his secret hiding places. He told Gran they contained special medial equipment and that she wasn't to touch them or snoop around. She had no reason to suspect anything.

Grandad had always promised me he was preparing me for life as a grown-up. Now I was at secondary school, I felt like a big girl. There was nothing much worse he could show me, I thought to myself.

Of course, I was wrong.

10. Indecent Acts

The scale of the abuse was becoming more savage by the day. Grandad would pin me on the bed, throttling me until I nearly blacked out. Being raped was bad enough, but being sadistically violently raped was beyond any horrific imaginings possible.

Under my school uniform I was covered in bruises and cuts from Grandad's abuse, but which my parents thought was a result of being bullied – as some of them were. The bullying at school had reached epic proportions and was a huge concern for my dad and other family members. The clique of girls who had picked on me at my old school had now really got it in for me. Before they'd picked on my ragged appearance, but now they changed tack. 'Pig's daughter,' they would spit at me as I walked through the playground. 'Such a little snob aren't you?' they'd taunt as I carried my violin case on my way to the orchestra. They didn't like the fact my dad was in the police force and we came from a well-to-do family. I never tried to defend myself, I knew there was no point. They'd slap me across the face with a stinging thwack, then all cackle with malicious laughter. Sometimes they flushed my head in the toilets, and once they even pushed me down the stairs. My parents frequently complained abut the bullying and the headmaster would call Dad every other week. He'd get the bullies excluded, but there wasn't much more he could do. Of course, the girls would come back from suspension and pick on me even more. In the end Dad lost patience with me saying, 'Emily, you *have* to fight back.' He didn't know I was too physically and psychologically broken on every level for that.

Once again, these events played into the hands of my grandfather – who often slapped me violently. All my bruises were blamed on the bullies, Dad had no reason to suspect it might be anyone else. If Grandad had attacked me badly, he would always order me to tell my father the bullies had been picking on me again. He didn't care what I was going through at school, he just wanted to use it to his own advantage. After all, he was doing far worse.

Dad came round for tea every so often. But he didn't stay for long, and we'd all sit round the dinner table and make small talk. There wasn't an opportunity for me to talk to him properly, so he never guessed. I'd ask after Lassie, worried she might be lonely or not being looked after properly, then I'd sink into a depression when he said she was well, and still enjoying her walks in the woods. It was built-up suburbia where Grandad lived, the house was in a maize of identical-looking houses, so crammed in on each other it was easy to get lost. Instead of trees I saw concrete now.

I missed the police house so much, with my little dog, my hidden dens in the countryside, and my super-psychedelic room that was repellent to grown-ups. Living at my grandparents' felt like death row in every way.

Grandad's obsession with me being 'grown up' kept taking ever more sickening turns. One night he arrived home with a new present for me. But this time it wasn't a rag doll, or a Barbie. It was large dildo, bought from a sex shop in the nearest town. It was shaped like a cucumber, the bottom containing liquid that could squirt out. For consenting adults it might have been a fun item, but for me it was another weapon of torture.

'What do you think of your big-girl gift?' he asked, smirking. He made me hold it, getting off on the sight of a little girl with such an indecent item.

I cast my eyes downwards, trying not to let him see my hands trembling as I held the monstrous thing.

My reactions to him veered between two extremes. Since I'd moved in with him and any semblance of normal life had ended, I had started to fight back when he attacked me. Before I'd been scared of what he might do, but now I was often pushed to such limits that my only option was to lash out. But perversely, he often enjoyed it when I went crazy, screaming and clawing at him in between my sobs. It turned him on. It also gave him an excuse to be even rougher with me. However much I struggled, he always won, and my pain was always twice as bad in the end. So sometimes I went to the other end of the spectrum, lying limply on the bed like a rag doll. I didn't want to give him the satisfaction of seeing how frightened and upset I was. It was my one little bit of control. He couldn't manipulate my reaction, so if I chose to be silent, he couldn't stop me.

But more often than not I struggled. It was a natural reaction: pain, anger and sheer panic often overwhelmed me. I felt I was fighting for my life.

The dynamic between me and Gran was also strained –

not that she realized it. Grandad set it up as though we were rivals when he spoke to me. At Christmas and birthdays, he'd buy Gran a present – a box of chocolates or something for the house usually. He'd whisper to me that I'd get a gift later, but that we mustn't make Gran jealous. As soon as she left the house he'd whip out a present in expensive-looking packaging for me. It was always something grown up like lingerie or perfume – the kind of gift a cheating husband might buy his mistress. For him, I was the bit on the side.

That night he made me spray on the rich, musky perfume he'd given me, so I left a heady scent wherever I walked. He'd bought me some slutty-looking red under-wear as a 'treat', and I pulled it on reluctantly on his orders.

Glancing in the mirror I saw a tragic, defeated look in my eyes – which appeared much older than my small twelve-year-old body. Gaudily tarted up, I looked like a child prostitute held against her will in a gruesome sex den. As I rolled the suspenders up my skinny legs I was careful not to press all the deep bruises and infected cuts along my inner thighs, testament to my numerous, previous ordeals that were taking place almost every night.

It was as if the twin personalities in my mind had manifested into two totally different people. Just that day at school I had performed in the orchestra, playing the violin. Wearing my smart school uniform, which, unlike Joan, Gran kept pristine, I must have looked like any other happy innocent little girl. I came from a nice family, played a musical instrument and probably played with my

Barbie when I got home. That's what onlookers would have thought. How wrong could they be?

'Are you ready?' shouted Grandad, his voice dulled with the regularity of what he was about to do. He only perked up when he walked into my room and spotted the dildo cast aside on the bed, and me trussed up in adult underwear. He had to push the boundaries of his perversions to still get excited. This is what really terrified me. It was always the same question I asked myself, with the same unspoken fear – *what next*?

From the start this question had fluttered round my mind like a trapped butterfly. Every time I concluded this was as bad as it could get, it got a whole lot worse. Somehow, at every stage, I managed to adjust to the new levels of pain and degradation just to survive. But now I felt that I was reaching the limits of what any human – let alone a small girl – could endure. There was a crisis coming, I could just feel it.

But would I survive it?

What continued to shock me more than anything was Grandad's deliberate cruelty. As I lay on the bed sniffling, shaking and begging for him to leave me alone, he just grimaced with glee. Because physically I was so tiny, he viewed all objects – from my hairbrush to the vile lump of plastic on the bed – as tools to prepare my body for the traumas to come.

This cucumber-shaped instrument of torture would become a firm favourite in his repertoire of evil. I imagined it was designed to be filled with lukewarm water. But that wouldn't do for my grandfather. Instead, he either filled it with freezing cold or boiling hot liquid –

both extremes that would have me writhing in pain, inflaming or stimulating all the previous wounds I had sustained in that area. My agony was his pleasure.

Tonight he seemed in a particularly sadistic mood, I don't know why. We never spoke of normal everyday things, and I had no clue what influenced him or stressed him out. He was a blank canvas to paint my fear on.

He offered me a tumbler of whisky, which was fuller than usual. I swallowed it down without questioning him, feeling woozy straight away. I was under five feet tall, so it went straight to my head immediately. Within minutes I knew I was in trouble. My head was spinning and I couldn't think straight. He loomed over me wielding the dildo, and then I realized what his intentions were.

I screamed and screamed and screamed, but the words sounded like a distant echo, far away. Alert enough to be aware of what was happening, I was too floppy to fight him off. I could still scream though.

'Please not that,' I begged, tears running down my face and gathering in rivulets down my neck. 'Please not that.'

I tried to push him off, but my hands were weaker than normal. It felt like using jelly to move concrete. He smirked, and lifted my arm up, smiling more widely as my wrist limply fell back on the bed.

'Trying to stop me, eh?' he gloated.

Then he began.

For the last few years he had taken to touching a different place to my flower. A bad place. I didn't really know why, I just knew that it was wrong. It felt dirtier than anything else he did – and it hurt far more.

Now he was preparing me, so he could do something

extremely unnatural to me. Suddenly a rip of pain tore through me, clearing the fog of alcohol and bringing me straight to my senses.

'No!' I screamed out, a piercing cry that carried through every room in the house. He pushed his hand over my mouth and angrily told me to shut up. I kicked him, not caring if he hit me. Nothing could be worse than this. 'No. No. No. No. No,' I almost chanted, like a mantra of pain.

After the cloudiness of before, everything was brought into sharp relief.

I fought and fought, but he was stronger than me. The pain was unspeakably bad. Like red-hot pokers ripping through me. Afterwards, I limped to the bathroom and wished I were already asleep. I just wanted to be in a place where all the hurt stopped and I could be at peace. But Grandad had other plans. Gran was on a catering course and wasn't coming back that night.

'Sleep in my bed with me,' he said gruffly.

I was too beaten and broken to argue. So I carefully removed my underwear, put my nightie on and climbed into his bed.

It felt so weird sleeping in their marriage bed, in the spot where Gran slept every night. I could smell her lavender perfume and Grandad's sweat ingrained on the sheets. He got into bed, and turned over with his back to me. I lay, looking at the ceiling, still shaking. Sleeping wasn't an option. After the atrocity of tonight, I was scared of what more he might do to me if I let my guard down and passed out.

The darkness in the room was oppressive. I felt it hang

over me like a cloud, choking me. I just wanted to be in my own bed.

I tossed and turned, sobbing and shaking.

'Go to sleep!' Grandad urged me, his voice sleepy and annoyed.

His little plan wasn't working out quite how he'd hoped.

By four o'clock he sat bolt upright and huffed, 'For God's sake go to your own bed, I haven't had a wink of sleep.'

Without a word I threw back the covers and scuttled back to my room with relief. There I felt I could give myself up to the darkness, letting it consume me, taking me to a land of dreams where fairies lived in trees and Lassie spoke to pixies in the woods when we'd lost our way.

The next morning I scrubbed my body all over with the metal brush. Blood streaked down my legs as I broke the skin with the force of it. But no matter what I did, I couldn't remove the feeling of dirtiness. Especially after what he'd done last night. I felt more desperate, more disassociated and numb than ever. So I just built my brick wall higher. I'd calculate I had at least ten hours, maybe twenty-four until he could hurt me again. Until then I was free. It was as though I had an internal timer, like a clock ticking, measuring how long until I would be in his clutches again. In this way, I broke my life down into manageable fragments of time so I could cope with the trauma.

Dad was so busy I didn't see much of him, and I felt abandoned by him. It proved Grandad was right as far as

I was concerned. My father wasn't to know what was happening, and because Grandad provided him with false reports that I was happy, he never questioned if I had settled in at my new home. But my behaviour had become more erratic than ever. I wasn't the cute little girl of the family any more, I was a moody, stroppy teenager.

When my grandfather took me on a drive I'd wear my headphones so I wouldn't have to listen to him, and if he spoke I'd pretend I hadn't heard. He would still drive me out into the middle of deserted countryside to abuse me, so my screams just carried on the wind, mingling with the cries of the gulls flying overhead to the seashore. But now I often fought back, turning my music up loud so I couldn't hear him scream angrily at me if I failed to obey him. It drove him wild with fury. He wanted to have total control over me, and hated it when I made any decisions for myself.

What I didn't know was that my rebellion, limited as it was, was about to have terrible consequences.

Because of my surly, non-compliant attitude, he decided he would have to make a radical change to the abuse: he would drug me.

I was still physically small, but the sexual acts he was forcing me into were becoming more extreme all the time. That, coupled with my newfound courage to fight back, meant drug-assisted rape would make things easier for him. This was where being a medically trained professional came in handy. He had access to strong prescription-only tranquillizers and painkillers, and he knew exactly the dosage required to knock someone out. So he twisted his medical expertise to get his way.

Part of my rebellion involved making up excuses to why he couldn't abuse me. I'd claim that I had period pains, or that my flower was sore from my last ordeal, or that I was coming down with a bad headache.

'My tummy's sore,' I'd beg, hoping he'd have some pity for me if I was ill.

I should have known better.

'Don't worry, I've got something to show you,' he said, the first time I tried this excuse.

It wasn't what I wanted to hear. Grandad's surprises were rarely pleasant. But I followed him as he strode towards his bedroom.

'This is my special drawer,' he told me, opening it with a flourish.

Peering in, I was bemused by strips of tablets with long, complicated names written onto them. The drawer was stuffed full of them.

I looked up at him bewildered.

Over the years, he had taken me on many visits to the ambulance station. He'd smile as he showed me bottles of medicine, tanks of gas and air and needles, ignoring my frightened expression. 'They are special medicines that put people to sleep if they're in pain,' he'd explained, looking menacingly towards me.

Now he was showing me 'special medicines' again, but this time they were kept at home, not in the ambulance. Once again, it confirmed his status to me. In the same way people automatically respect doctors, I thought it showed how important he was, that he had all these prescription tablets in the house.

It never occurred to me why he might need so many drugs at home.

'This'll take the pain away,' he said, assuming his authoritative doctor-type voice, and popping three large pink pills out of the packet. He didn't hand them to me straight away. Instead, he told me to wait in my bedroom, then walked downstairs to the living room.

Within minutes he was back, carrying a large tumbler of gin.

'Drink it down all in one!' he ordered me.

'I don't want to,' I protested, sensing that something wasn't right, but not knowing why.

He glowered at me, his eyes screwing up into tiny balls of fury.

'Do as I say ... or I'll tell your dad you've been bad and he'll lock you up in the police cell,' he threatened menacingly.

I hesitated, then took the glass and swigged it back, popping the pills into my mouth. They stuck in my throat, leaving a bitter artificial taste, and I shuddered as I tried to wash them down.

Grandad was watching intently, as though he was embarking on a new experiment. I stared back at him, still trying to choke down the remnants of the sickly-tasting tablets and coughing at the sharp sting of the gin in my stomach.

A few minutes of unbearable silence passed.

Our eyes rarely met for long, but this time we held each other's gaze. The moment lasted a long time, stretching on longer and longer. Time had gained an unexpected elasticity. My insides were doing unusual things too. I felt as though my mind could slip out of my body, like a drink spilling over the edges of my existence. It was strange, and I didn't like it. I had to lie down. Falling back on the bed, I tried to tell Grandad how tired I was, but I couldn't speak, no matter how hard I tried. It felt like being in a bad dream, when you lose the faculty of speech. I could still focus on his eyes, which were shining unnaturally in the light, boring into me. If I looked too hard at them they started to spin round, faster and faster, like a demented Catherine wheel.

Get a grip, I told myself fearfully.

Losing control like this was terrifying. I needed to be alert, to be on guard against Grandad. Even if I couldn't stop what he was doing, I could make sure that every cell of my body was screaming with resistance, so I could put my emotions and my remaining purity in my safe place.

But I felt like I was falling down the sheer face of a cliff with nothing to cling on to. For a few seconds I could scramble back into consciousness, and then my grip would loosen again and I'd be plummeting down-wards into the darkness. It was a terrible conflict: my own will to remain awake, and something unknown inside me pulling me under towards oblivion. It wasn't like falling asleep, where you drifted peacefully into another world. This was like being sucked in against your will, at speed.

Then I heard the birds singing excitedly outside my window, and the heat of the sun shining through the curtains. It was morning.

My head felt hazy, and for a moment I had to think hard about where I was. I wondered if, like Alice in

Wonderland, I had fallen down a hole and into another world.

I peeled open one eye, and a subdued star twinkled above me on the ceiling.

Looking to the side I saw my wardrobe, and my rag doll propped against it at a jaunty angle, her blonde hair a vivid yellow against the white wood.

What had happened to me? Fear raced through my mind.

I couldn't remember anything.

It was like trying to recall a dream upon waking. The second you think you have the memory, it slips away from you – but still close enough to taunt you with its presence on the periphery of your consciousness.

But if my mind was a blank, the same couldn't be said for my body.

Trying to roll over, I instantly groaned in pain. Feeling hurt the next day was nothing new to me, but this was different. My body felt different, but I just couldn't remember why. The *not knowing* suddenly seemed more terrible than the visions of the night before I was usually haunted by. You can try and come to terms with a memory, but endless awful possibilities don't allow for any kind of emotional closure. It's hard to forget a question mark hanging over you.

Between my legs was *really* sore. My pelvis hurt when I moved too. My legs were wracked with the intense pain similar to when I'd overdone it in PE class, and pushed my body too far, pulling all the muscles.

Something bad had happened, I just didn't know what.

Maybe it's better this way, I told myself. Slowly I eased

myself up onto my pillows, taking sharp inhalations every time part of my bruised body came into contact with the bed.

As always Grandad said nothing, acting as if everything was normal. But he had a sick glint in his eye – like a spoilt kid who has a new toy and has worked out a way to keep it all to himself. He saw me struggle to walk down the stairs to breakfast, but he didn't care.

It was like living with a serial killer who has decided to murder you slowly. The coldness and lack of emotion in his eyes was scarier than anything.

They say that one of the first rules of torture is to surprise victims, never giving them any type of routine to cling onto. Grandad was a genius at this.

The next night I had it all worked out. I would refuse the tablets, then if he made me take them, I would only pretend to swallow them, spitting them out when I could. If I'd lost consciousness then it was as though he was raping a dead person, I thought to myself. I wanted to die, but while I was still breathing, the least respect he could give me was to treat me as if I was alive.

Sitting in my room all psyched up, I heard him pound-ing up the stairs. But rather than come in, he stopped, climbed on his footstool, and peered in at me through the window. This always unnerved me, and he knew it.

He enjoyed these sick mind games, and this signalled he was in a more sadistic mood than normal. A few minutes later he walked in through the door with his usual implements of torture in his hand. I steeled myself for a bad night. For a second my mind drifted to thoughts of the police house. Would Lassie be warming herself in front of the fire until her fur smelled slightly singed as usual? Would the wind whistle through the woodlands, with the boats in the harbour knocking against each other in rhythmic percussion? There was a fairyland just out of my reach, and I was trapped in the castle.

I braced myself to refuse his evil potion, but then Grandad did something unexpected. He turned his back to me and started fiddling with the karaoke machine in the corner of the room. I leaned forward to see what he was doing. No matter how beaten I was, there was no way I was going to sing the soundtrack to my own sexual abuse, I thought to myself darkly. He was inserting a cassette, I noticed with curiosity. The machine had a facility to tape people singing, to keep your performance for posterity.

Grandad pushed record, then pushed me onto the bed.

He didn't want to drug me tonight. He wanted to hear my screams. But not only did he want to hear them – he wanted to record them. It must have been a dilemma for him. Drug-rape me, and have a free hand to inflict extreme perversions on me with no resistance, or have me conscious so he could enjoy my hysterical pleas for mercy. Tonight he wanted to hear me beg for him to stop. And he wanted to be able to enjoy that pleasure over and over again.

Who could listen to a tape like that? With the sound of him threatening me, instructing me what to do and how he wanted me, alongside the desperate sounds of my sobs, pleas and wails, sometimes hushed with pain, sometimes high and hysterical with fear. But who would listen to it and be aroused by it? My grandad's perversion had now become a form of insanity.

To make sure he recorded a good 'performance' he treated me even more roughly than usual, pushing me until my piercing screams bounced off the walls. Grabbing my throat, he almost throttled me, telling me to beg him to stop. I felt I was pleading for my life. Terrified, I couldn't help but fulfil his sick plan and sob for him to stop.

Afterwards, he left me collapsed on the bed, shaking with terror. He wasn't bothered about me at all – I was just a prop in his disgusting plan. He pulled the cassette out triumphantly, and held it tightly in his big calloused hands. The satisfied look on his face was obscene. It was a big risk for him to record what he was doing. But he was so crazed he was prepared to risk everything to get bigger thrills.

He was out of control.

11. Dark Secrets

I had become a keeper of secrets. There were so many stories I had to store inside me, it became easier to swallow them down rather than speak up. The horrors were too great and the incidents too many for me ever to find the words to describe them – or the faith that anyone would believe me. My secrets were folded like a concertina inside me, contracting until finally the springs would push them out with great force.

But that moment was a long way off. For now, silence was my friend.

There was one more secret too which I hadn't told *anybody*. Not even Lassie.

Somebody else had also sexually assaulted me.

It was something I'd pushed out of my mind for two years, but now it was about to come back and haunt me. Like most things, it ended up working in Grandad's favour. It was as though he was a great puppeteer pulling all the strings.

It happened on my tenth birthday, not long after I'd moved into the police station. Dad and Joan had organized a fancy birthday party for me at the local church hall. I think they were pulling out all the stops to win me over. All the kids from the village had been invited, and there was a trestle table loaded with fairy cakes, jelly, crisps and sandwiches. I was all dressed up in a pretty red tartan dress with a matching red satin sash tied around the waist, black tights and shiny black patent-leather shoes. I felt like a proper princess.

Dad had really gone to town on my party, and every time he came over for a hug, I beamed back at him, feeling dizzy with happiness. So far, it had been one of the best days of my life. For once, I could put all the misery of what Grandad was doing to me out of my mind.

My birthday cake was decorated with ten pink candles, which I blew out with gusto, wishing that this day could never end.

Afterwards, all the kids were given a slice of cake to take home, along with a party bag, filled with trinkets, like balloons, fake nails, yo-yos and sweets.

I twirled round, singing to myself and bouncing about, full of energy, in total attention-seeking mode. This was *my* day, I thought proudly to myself. But there was one glitch. My new friend, Mary, had been too ill to come. Maybe it was because my life was so full of suffering that I was acutely sensitive to the pain or sadness of other people. I felt really bad for Mary that she'd missed out. I couldn't get the image of her lying poorly in bed while we were having such fun out of my mind. There was also another reason I was sorry for her: she was new to the area, and I guessed she'd been looking forward to today, hoping she would get to know more local kids. I understood how hard it was to make friends, so my heart really went out to her. We'd bonded because we were both outsiders, but I didn't want her to share my lonely fate. I wouldn't wish that on anyone.

The adults were packing everything away, and most of

the children were waving goodbye as their mums came to pick them up. I knew most of them wouldn't want to know me by Monday morning. Kids can be horribly fickle like that. But I lived one day at a time, so it was enough for me that at least for today I'd felt what it was like to be popular without being picked on.

With everything winding up, we remaining kids were bored. It was still only three o'clock on Saturday afternoon. Suddenly I had a brainwave.

'Let's take Mary a party bag,' I said to my cousin Ally, who was a year younger than me, grabbing her hands with enthusiasm, jigging around at the brilliance of my plan.

It would be nice to make Mary's day, and we could have an adventure too.

Ally was a real tomboy, chalk to my cheese. She'd come to the party wearing jeans, sensible boots and a T-shirt. As I suspected, she was instantly up for my plan, shouting, 'Yeahhh!' with excitement.

I asked Joan if we were allowed to go and she waved us off, passing me an extra party bag for Mary. She was glad to have me out of her hair for a few hours. As far as she was concerned, she'd done her good stepmum bit for the year. Being such a rural, close-knit village, it wasn't unusual for children to wander around the local countryside on their own. What danger could there be?

We set off, but there was one problem. We didn't actually know where the house was. We *kind of* knew, but we weren't exactly sure. One thing we did know though was that Mary lived in the biggest, most expensive house in the area. We'd seen it from a distance before, perched on the hill, looking over the forests and rivers, made almost entirely out of glass, like a modernist cube nestled among ancient woodlands. It even had its own stables and a helicopter pad. How could we miss it?

Feeling confident we could easily find our way there, we strolled along, nibbling on cake and chattering loudly. But as we walked up a deserted road, listening to the whispering of the trees surrounding us, we got scared, quieting our conversation to a hush.

'It's a bit creepy up here, isn't it?' whispered Ally with a nervous giggle.

I said nothing, but quickened my pace. The trees were leaning in, forming a canopy of green over our heads. Suddenly we reached a fork in the road.

On the path that we imagined led to the house was a big sign, 'Private Path'. We looked at each other, unsure what to do.

'We can't go up there, it's private,' I said to Ally. We'd been well brought up, and were too scared to trespass when a sign told us we couldn't.

She scuffed her boot into the mud at the side of the road, squinted at the forbidden road, and agreed. 'What shall we do?' she asked.

The other path led to the grounds of a luxury country hotel. I pointed in that direction and replied, 'Let's go this way.'

We felt safer, and planned to ask someone at the hotel to help us. Holding hands, we innocently skipped along, glad we'd passed the scary bit. Ahead of us we could see stables, with the velvety brown noses of horse sticking out, sniffing the spring day. There was a guy tending them. He looked about nineteen. Average-looking, with thick black hair.

He grinned in a friendly manner when he saw us standing there.

'Can I help you, girls?' he shouted over, wiping his hands down the sides of his jeans, and walking towards us.

'We're lost!' shouted back Ally. 'Can you help?'

Pointing back down the way we'd come from, we explained we couldn't get to where we were going because of a private road. We could actually see the house now, on the hill above us, its glass walls glinting in the sun like sparkling diamonds. The guy looked up at the house, and cocked his head at an angle. 'I reckon your best bet is over this field here,' he told us, looking straight ahead. 'You'll be all right,' he said to Ally, 'but I'm not sure she'll make it over in that outfit.' He chuckled to himself after he spoke.

I looked down at my fancy party dress and blushed.

'Don't worry,' he reassured me in a kinder voice. 'I'll give you a piggy back so you don't have to ruin your pretty party shoes.'

Looking up at the house, I worked out that if we managed to cross the field, we were almost there, so I agreed.

Ally jumped over the fence in front of us, and I perched on the top, too nervous to jump down. The stable boy crouched in front of me and told me to hop on. So I clambered on his back, just like I did when my brother Tom carried me round. I felt perfectly at ease, with no worries.

Because of Grandad, I was naturally frightened of men. But to me, this guy was just a boy, just like my brothers and stepbrothers.

Straight away his hands grabbed hold of my bum. It

made me feel uncomfortable, but I reasoned that he was doing it to keep me on. Tom sometimes did the same when I was sliding off. But it didn't feel the same.

At the end of the muddy, brambly field he put me down. His expression had changed. He no longer looked liked a harmless stable boy. There was something leery about the way he stared at me, and his manner was nervous. I gulped with fear – it was a look I knew only too well.

The silence of the fields became frightening, like a blanket resting over everything, smothering us. Ally said nothing. But I could see she was shaking. Like me, she instantly sensed that something was deeply wrong.

'You're an awfully pretty girl,' he drawled, walking towards me. Even though he was young, he was tall. Stood over me, I finally felt the force of his power as a man – something I had missed before, classing him as a boy.

He grabbed my arm roughly, his fingers sinking into my skin. With the other hand he pushed my dress up and yanked down my pants. I was too shocked and scared to say anything. Ally was trembling with fear, standing rooted to the spot in stunned silence, just watching the scene unfold.

The sexual assault was quick, unlike with Grandad. I knew there was no point in running, and besides, his grip on my arm was too strong.

After a few painful, terrifying moments, Ally suddenly blurted out, 'We have to go now, my mum and dad are waiting for me.'

Startled, he looked at her, then started to back off,

breaking into a run. He didn't have Grandad's nerve; he lost his confidence and bolted.

Ally was sobbing, clearly thinking she would have been next. Tears were streaming down my face too, but for more complicated reasons. In a strange way, I was relieved. Knowing what I did about the pain and damage a man could inflict on a little girl, I was glad it hadn't been worse. But I was also terrified, and shaken beyond belief. As soon as the ordeal had started those same words had popped into my mind. *What next?* I had been convinced he would rape both of us. That's what men did. It also reinforced everything Grandad said, that what he did was normal. He often claimed that all men did it to little girls to help them grow up.

Was he right? I wondered to myself, crying and fixing my dress back in place. It felt like there was a sick secret code that all men shared.

Without saying a word, we both broke into a sprint, racing through brambles, which cut our legs, and pushing branches out of our way. Within minutes we arrived at the door of Mary's house. All along, we had been close to safety. Our hearts pounding in our chests, and our breath still shuddering, we pressed the bell violently, with growing hysteria.

Ally kept looking back over her shoulder saying, 'What if he comes back?'

There was no answer at the door. They must have gone out. Maybe they'd taken Mary to the doctor's.

Abandoning the party bag on the step, so the sweets spilled out in candy-coloured disarray, we looked round wildly for our escape route. We couldn't go back the way we'd come. We were convinced he was waiting for us. Sobbing, we hugged each other for a second and then both agreed. 'Let's take the private path,' we said simultaneously. Running together, trying to hold hands, we staggered down the path. We must have looked an odd sight – Ally in her blue jeans, and me in my bright dress. The wind in the trees made noises like monsters rustling in the undergrowth, waiting to attack us, and we often screamed out loud, only to hush each other. 'He might hear us,' I cautioned Ally in a cross whisper.

When we finally hit the main road, we slowed down. Finally we spoke about what had happened. For Ally, it was the first time in her life she had realized men could do bad things. Sadly, I already knew that all too well.

'We've *got* to tell,' was her first reaction.

That thought panicked me. She didn't understand that secrets *had* to be kept. If anyone found out, I would be sent away. My hands started shaking badly.

'No, please don't say anything,' I begged her. 'My dad will be really angry with me.'

She looked at me puzzled, what I was saying didn't make sense to her. But thanks to years of malicious grooming, it made perfect sense to me.

'He's the bad one.'

'You don't understand,' I tried to explain, crying my eyes out. 'I'll be in really bad trouble if anyone finds out about this.'

It's tragic to realize that if Grandad hadn't been in my life, I would have rushed straight home to tell my dad. But I was preconditioned to expect men to sexually abuse me, and if all men did this, who would really care, even if I did tell anyone? I'd gain nothing and probably lose everything.

In the end Ally promised to keep quiet, and my sobbing calmed down. So we made a pact, to never mention it to *anyone*. No doubt she decided it was my secret to keep. It was never spoken about again. Until two years later.

In that time my life had changed dramatically – all for the worse.

Now here I was, twelve years old, with Grandad dressing me up as a plaything, drug-raping me, and much worse. The fun of my tenth birthday party, and the shocking assault that took place after it, all seemed like a lifetime away.

Luckily, shortly after I got a reprieve from my misery – a week at Guide camp.

Even though I'm sure he didn't want to lose a week of abusing me, there was nothing Grandad could say when I asked my dad if I could go and he said yes.

Dressed in my smart blue uniform, wearing a yellow tie, with badges sewn all down my sleeves, announcing I was proficient in everything from baking and needlework to lighting fires, I set off.

I couldn't quite believe my luck. A whole week without him. Usually, twenty-four hours was the longest I ever went between assaults. Now I had an entire 168 hours of freedom and knowing I was safe.

Better still, we would be camping in a forest, making fires and gallivanting around under the clear blue skies. Being close to nature made me happy. It was the opposite of the claustrophobic, cramped-together houses on Grandad's estate. Out in the wilds, there was a sense of escape and exhilaration. I'd spent my life feeling trapped – here I felt free. I loved having the space to breathe. It made me realize how, in my normal life, I was curled up in a ball of unimaginable tension. I was constantly bracing myself against attack, like an animal on red alert.

After a few days unwinding, collecting firewood and singing silly songs by the fire at night, I decided to call Dad and tell him what a great time I was having. All the other kids were making calls to their parents, and the paranoid side of me worried that my family had forgotten I existed. I always felt my grip on any love in my life was tenuous, and should be held onto tightly. Feeling alone and unwanted was the worst pain of all.

There was a pay phone on the campsite and I queued up with a few coppers in my hand, waiting in line for my turn to speak.

The receiver was heavy in my hand, not like the light plastic one at home. I dialled Dad's number, but it rang and rang and no one answered. I sighed with disappointment. Turning round, I could see other girls queuing to speak to their loved ones. I didn't want them to think no one cared about me, so I decided to call Gran. I don't know why, I just assumed she'd be the one who answered – at home she always picked up the phone first.

After a brief dialling tone, a voice said hello. It was Grandad. A flood of nausea washed over me just at the sound of his voice. For a second my head started spinning. Then I collected myself, and in a little voice said, 'Hello.'

'Listen carefully,' he said in strange tone of voice. It had a tinge of panic I had never heard before. 'I know you don't have much time to talk.'

I fed another copper two-pence piece into the phone, listening with rising fear, wondering what this was all about.

'I'm listening,' I replied meekly.

'I need to talk to you; this is serious,' he said quickly, his words tripping over each other as he tried to speed the conversation on. 'Your cousin has told about the lad in the village who touched you,' he said bluntly. It felt like an accusation.

My stomach flip-flopped, and my legs wobbled. This was finally it, I was going to be sent away for ever, I thought in absolute panic.

'When you get home, the police will be waiting for you – to take you away,' he continued. The way he worded it, it was as if I'd be the one sent to prison, not the stable boy who had hurt me. It felt like it was all my fault.

'I don't want to be arrested,' I gulped down the phone.

'Well, you're going to have to tell them your cousin's lying then.'

'But she's not lying,' I replied, with conviction. 'It *did* happen.'

In my childish way, now the secret was out, I felt I should tell the truth.

'Look, they'll do tests and examine you and find out about our little secret,' Grandad hissed down the phone. 'Then you really will be sent away.'

I pushed another coin into the slot and tried to hold back my tears.

'Everyone will believe me, not you,' he carried on, his words coming out quickly, like rapid gunfire. 'No one wants you, nobody cares about you – haven't you realized that by now? Your mum didn't want you, and neither did your dad. If they found out about this, there's nothing more I can do. You'll be sent away. Everyone will hate you for ever.' He paused, and there was a moment of silence on the line. 'What are you going to say to them, then?' he asked harshly.

'I'll tell them she's lying,' I promised in a barely audible whisper.

'Good girl,' Grandad said, sounding relieved. His voice was back to normal.

Then the phone clicked dead. My money had run out.

I passed the phone to the next girl, feeling dazed.

Dragging my feet in despair, I sat down on a low wall nearby. I watched, tears streaming quietly down my face, as other girls chattered to their parents, swapping 'love yous' at the end, often a few times.

Even though Dad would hug me and say he loved me, I suspected he didn't. How could he? Grandad was right. Just like Mum, he'd sent me away.

People who claimed to love me always hurt me. By now the line between love and hurt was so blurred it had become the same thing – betrayal.

Suddenly I felt very far away from home. Even though home was hell, this aloneness was even worse. But I was terrified to go back too.

My mind raced round and round, not knowing which way to turn.

I imagined a world where I had a proper grandad. He

would have reassured me, saying, 'Don't worry, sweetie, just tell the truth.'

That Grandad didn't exist.

At the end of camp, the Guide leaders dropped me off at the local church hall. Joan picked me up. She didn't suspect I already knew my secret was out. Of course, I never mentioned the phone call with Grandad. Before she even switched the engine on, she looked at me and said, 'We need to have a little talk.'

I asked why, without much conviction. I already knew.

We drove in silence, and when I got to the police station, Dad said I should go and wait in my old room. He spoke gently, trying not to alarm me.

'Something serious has happened, and you need to be a big girl,' he told me. Without knowing it, he was using the same terms Grandad did, reinforcing his evil message to me. But he didn't question me about the allegations. As a policeman he knew not to speak to me before his colleagues had arrived to interview me formally.

Joan brought me up a glass of milk and a biscuit, setting it down silently on the bedside table. It felt weird to watch the psychedelic patterns on the walls again. It depressed me. Lassie was out with my brothers, so she couldn't console me. I heard the door click downstairs, and the sound of grown-up voices discussing things in serious tones.

The police were here, and I was terrified. I couldn't stop thinking about the cell below me, and how they might lock me up in there.

It was as if a strange veil passed down over my eyes

seconds before the police came upstairs. The mask slipped on. My reasoning was twisted so much by Grandad that I half suspected they were trying to trick me into confessing, just so they could lock me up or send me away. I absolutely believed I was in the wrong and they were trying to catch me out.

To my surprise, a dainty-looking policewoman walked in. She knelt down in front of me, placing herself at my eye level.

'Your cousin has told us what happened, now we need you to tell us,' she said softly, with a kind look in her eye.

I looked down and fidgeted with the hem of my skirt.

She carried on talking, trying to coax it out of me. 'If something *did* happen, we'll do something about it,' she assured me earnestly. 'And don't worry, it's not you who'll get into trouble. It's bad to touch a little girl; he'll be punished,' she added.

My eyes widened in surprise. Alarm bells went off in my head: what she was saying didn't make sense. *I* was the one in trouble.

'We'll make sure it doesn't happen again and that he can't do it to you or anyone else,' she continued.

By now something had switched in my mind, and as far as I was concerned, we were having a conversation about my grandad. Everything the police lady was saying was wrong. Grandad could do it to any little girl he wanted to – he'd told me that often enough. *No one* could stop him, I was sure of that.

'It didn't happen,' I said firmly, shaking my head and staring at my shoes. 'My cousin's fibbing,' I added, just like Grandad had told me to.

Eventually, she gave up trying to persuade me to talk. 'I don't believe you,' she told me in a resigned voice. 'I think you're very afraid, and if you ever feel ready to tell us, please remember you won't get in trouble.'

She left the room with a quiet sigh. Downstairs she told Dad that she thought I had been attacked, but that they couldn't do anything unless I made a statement. For the next few days he kept trying to talk to me about it, telling me I needed to tell the truth, but eventually he gave up.

After the initial fuss had died down, it got swept under the carpet.

Grandad was very pleased with me. 'You've done the right thing,' he said smugly, dragging on a cigarette when I went back to his house. 'Things could be a whole lot worse if you got sent away.'

He looked like a man celebrating victory. He knocked back his whisky with a satisfied noise and gave me a lecture on why I must always keep his secret.

The events had worked to his advantage on many levels. Firstly, he used the fact that I had lied to the police against me – even though he had made me.

'They'll never believe anything you say now,' he said gleefully. 'You're a liar, and if you go to them again, they'll arrest you for making a false statement. I'll let them know you lied, don't worry about that.'

Grandad's logic was perverse, but it worked on me. I realized I had somehow shot myself in the foot. I still felt it was the only option I'd had, but I knew it had closed a door on me ever confessing what Grandad was doing.

Secondly, he felt more confident that if the police ever did get suspicious about him, he could manipulate me into lying to cover for him. Also, it was less likely Dad would ask awkward questions about my behaviour. Before, everyone had put my strange moods down to the divorce, but now they had a new reason to hang my problems onto.

Years later, I discovered my cousin had blurted our secret out after hearing her mum and Joan gossip about why I was such a strange kid. It had been Ally's way of sticking up for me, trying to provide an explanation. But now it stopped anyone digging for anything deeper.

My *real* secret was safe.

After it was over, the words of the policewoman came back into my mind as I lay in bed after my frequent ordeals: 'It's bad to touch little girls.'

Suddenly everything in my head became jumbled. Part of me still thought they were trying to trick me, but another part whispered to me, in an alluring voice, telling me that Grandad was the only person to have told me what he was doing was normal and that no one loved me. Maybe *he* was lying, not the police . . .

I put it out of my mind, but it kept nagging away at me. Like a kettle, a first a few bubbles of anger surfaced inside me, but year after year, rape after rape, that anger boiled into a rage. The worse it became, the stronger I got.

It was fight or flight syndrome: I *had* to survive.

12. Too Much to Bear

The angrier I became, the greater the force Grandad used against me. If I cried he'd slap me across the face or thrash my legs, his big gold rings cutting the skin open. He alternated between enjoying the fight, to using drugs to subdue me into submission. In his 'special' shelf, stored alongside his vile sex toys, was a bottle of liquid he told me was chloroform – a dangerous drug that suppresses the nervous system, causing loss of consciousness. Whatever it was, he now used it on me as well as the tablets.

If I ever complained of a sniffle, he'd douse a handkerchief in the liquid, then press it tightly over my mouth and nose so I could barely breathe. Within seconds everything would start spinning, then I would be out cold. I could only imagine what he'd done to me in those hours of oblivion. The pain I suffered the next day was my only clue. But depraved as these acts were, they still didn't go far enough to satisfy my grandad's sick lusts – he wanted to go further.

I was just turned thirteen, but despite the abuse I was very young for my age. I still escaped into a dream world and played the same games I had done since childhood. Unlike most other teenage girls, I wasn't interested in growing up and discovering boys and sex. When Grandad wasn't violating me, I wanted to keep everything as pure and innocent as possible.

When summer came I liked to play out in the garden. I'd lay a bath towel out on the grass and sit in the sunshine, with all my dolls lined up and a wee radio to sing along to. Annie Lennox was my favourite, and I'd hum along to her songs, swinging my ponytail from side to side. I'd often write the lyrics down in my large elaborate handwriting, and design little doodles, alongside drawings of fairy castles and princesses in swirling dresses. They say abuse shows in the pictures you create, but there were no classic signs in mine – I didn't draw a bogie man with black crayons. Instead, I escaped from the horror of my life with fantasy. My pictures were brightly coloured flights of fancy. To the outside world, I looked like a girl with an over-active imagination. No one realized it was my way of trying to escape. Anyway, they wouldn't have guessed I had anyone to escape from.

Grandad was a keen gardener, which reinforced his image as a wholesome man. He spent lots of his time pottering about, growing vegetables and tending his flowers. He grew herbs, tomatoes and other veg in season, often taking baskets round to the neighbours. If he went up to the farm, he'd always come back with fresh eggs he'd collected and hand them out among the community. He must have appeared like such a solid, respectable man. That's how people are judged in suburbia. The flower-beds were beautifully kept, bursting with blushing pink carnations, red snapdragons, velvety pansies and bright marigolds. In this world, people were judged on their 'respectability' – and Grandad was upstanding.

No one suspected the beast he was behind closed doors.

But in his arrogance, Grandad started to dice with his reputation, feeling sure no one would catch him out. It was the biggest thrill of all.

One day, as I was playing in the sun, he stood staring at me from the window. 'Why don't you run upstairs and put your bathing costume on?' he shouted, saying that I'd be too hot in my dress.

I dashed upstairs to put my pink swimming costume on. I loved the frill that trimmed the bottom, so I twirled round, pretending I was a mermaid.

I never questioned his motives. He was right – it was roasting hot.

Looking back, that's what disturbs me most. How he twisted these innocent moments into evil – and I never suspected a thing. Time and time again, I only saw the trap when it was too late.

'Why don't you sit on a sunlounger?' he suggested when I came back outside. They were big, blue chrome beds too heavy for me to move; he'd positioned one to face the patio windows.

'I want to play on the grass,' I replied smiling, kneeling by the flowerbed and digging with my toy spade, just like I watched Grandad do.

'No, you should have a rest on the sunbed,' he replied. By his tone of voice I knew this was a command not a suggestion.

I padded over to the sunlounger in my bare feet and lay down. Instantly I felt uncomfortable. Gran always sunbathed on them, and they felt too grown-up for me. Grandad retreated inside, to shelter from the sun I presumed.

Before long I looked up and saw him watching me through the window. I felt that terrible creepy feeling, like a million spiders crawling all over you.

After a few moments he knocked on the window and signalled for me to come in. It was Saturday afternoon, and Gran was already at work, so we were alone together. Alarm bells started to ring.

'I've been sitting watching you,' he told me with a steel edge to his voice. 'I want you to go out and pull your costume to the side – I want to see how grown-up you are.'

'No, I don't want to do that,' I blurted out. The thought of it made me feel ashamed. Houses overlooked the garden, and it felt as though eyes were staring in, watching. What if anyone saw me? As a teenager I was very aware of my body. I'd started to get budding breasts, which made me feel self-conscious. Grandad would often try and toss water over me, making my costume clingy, making me feel ashamed and dirty about being on display. I really, really didn't want to do this.

'Get out there and push that costume to the side,' he snarled in my face, 'or else I'll call your dad and get the police to take you away.'

Terrified, I walked outside and did as I was told.

I felt so ashamed. What if the neighbours are looking? I thought, worrying they'd think I hadn't covered myself properly.

Grandad peered out at me, looking into my most intimate places.

By making me expose myself in public, it was as if he was testing how far he could go before he got caught. He was enjoying the sense of voyeurism. Now, men pay women to watch them undress on a webcam. This was his version of doing that, except I was under age, and this was incest. I worried other men were looking at me too, and this deepened my shame. Part of me wondered if Grandad had alerted other men to what was happening, inviting them to share in this private viewing.

Little did I know how accurate this premonition was.

At first, I only moved my costume to the side a little. Then he signalled frantically for me to move it more. I inched it a millimetre across.

He walked out on the pretence of giving me a drink and hissed, 'That's not enough, move it again.'

Shaking, I did exactly as he told me.

Through the window I could see him watching me, and masturbating.

He wasn't even being discreet. As always he was dressed immaculately, wearing black dress trousers and a shirt – I never saw him wear jeans. His formal dress asserted his sense of authority, but with his trousers unbuttoned, he looked like the sick degenerate he really was. It was as though he were testing the waters. Every time he got away with something, it proved that he could take things further. The more he thought he wouldn't get found out, the more daring he became. He was a paramedic, and his son was a policeman – who would believe them if anyone said anything? He thought he was absolutely bulletproof.

Suddenly it was over, and he beckoned me inside to tell me he was done.

I knew enough by now to realize that he wouldn't

attack me. He'd got what he wanted already. I felt dirty and ashamed at what he'd made me do, but it was better than the pain of rape, I thought to console myself.

I ran inside, and made my way straight up the stairs, slamming my door behind me. Grandad, stomped up the stairs after me.

'Go and play outside,' he told me.

'No! I won't!' I shouted back, throwing myself on the bed. I refused to go outside. I was too humiliated after what Grandad had made me do.

Realizing he couldn't persuade me, he gave up trying and shrugged his shoulders with annoyance, saying, 'What's wrong with you?'

'What if someone else saw?' I asked, biting the side of my thumbnail.

'Don't worry. If they did watch, they'd just see what a big girl you were,' he said flippantly, like it was no big deal. As he left my room, he turned round and gave me a knowing grin. 'Anyway, I've got a friend who would really like you.'

He closed the door behind him, but the threat hung in the air.

Peeking out of the window, I was convinced people had seen. I became paranoid that they were watching me in a silent accusation of shame. Crying, I fled to the bathroom to try and scrub myself clean. The metal spokes on the brush scratched and tore my skin. Strangely, this sensation was the only feeling that made the real pain disappear.

But a new fear whirred round my head. What friend? What did he mean? I suspected all men were like this –

the sexual assault by the stable boy had confirmed that. Was there a network of perverts Grandad belonged to?

Over the next few days he spelt it out to me. Sitting in his special chair, puffing away on his cigarette, he informed me that he was going to introduce me to all his friends. He talked as if I were an object he could pass around.

'Bob would love to see you in your suspenders,' he said, with a leering laugh. 'You can doll yourself up in all your sexy underwear.'

He went on to name lots of friends who would be interested in me. He described them all as people in positions of authority – policemen, firemen, paramedics. He really knew how to mess with my mind.

I froze with horror as he spoke. This wasn't something I could dismiss as an idle threat. After all, everything my grandad told me eventually came true. He was like the oracle of doom. I trembled with terror as he talked.

But after a few days, I tried to put the thought out of my mind. Otherwise, it would send me mad with fear. I just hoped he was lying.

Then one day I came home from school and found we had a visitor.

Gran was out at work, so there was no one at home to protect me.

As soon as I walked in and saw Grandad's friend sitting awkwardly in Grandad's chair, I just *knew*. It's hard to explain the feeling, like a sudden sinking in the pit of your stomach, sucking everything downwards with unstoppable fear. The shock was so great, I wobbled, a little unsteady on my feet. Then carefully I put my school-bag down on the dining table. My movements were slow, like I was frightened of triggering a hidden device, which might blow up in my face. The room smelt of old men, cheap aftershave mixed with stale sweat. Grandad was sat on the sofa, which struck me as unusual.

'Come and sit on my knee and give me a hug?' he coaxed me in a false, sickly-sweet voice. I knew he was putting on a show, but immediately my mask of politeness went up. I didn't want to cause a scene in front of a stranger, so I tiptoed across the carpet and sat tentatively on the edge of his knee. Still moving with the quiet stealth of somebody expecting a surprise attack, every bone in my body was seized with terrified expectation.

'You should see under her vest, she's getting proper grown up,' Grandad remarked to his friend, as if he were merely exchanging pleasantries.

Then he pushed his hands up my school shirt and starting touching me under my vest. In my head, the bomb exploded. As soon as he started touching me, in front of his friend, I knew beyond doubt what he planned. I'd spent the last week gripped with anxiety that some-one had seen me sunbathing, or that he would introduce me to his friends. Now it was actually happening. My lower lip quivered, and I clenched my little fists tight with fear.

His friend said nothing. He looked even more disgust-ing than Grandad. He was much older, wearing grey trousers and a grey jumper. The bald patch on top of his head was barely disguised by the few strands of greasy white hair threaded round in a pathetic coil. He looked like the stereotypical dirty old man in a raincoat, with a pungent smell surrounding him.

'I'll show you how it's done,' my grandad said, as if he was reading an instruction manual. He started to take my clothes off, removing my school blazer clumsily first, then removing every item until I was naked. I started to cry and tried to cover myself up.

He said, 'Don't be so stupid – you're all grown-up now. It's about time you showed someone else how grown-up you are.'

I shook my head and sobbed a silent no. Grabbing my wrists, he hissed, 'You know what's going to happen,' and pushed me onto the sofa.

Until then, his friend had sat in silence, clearly feeling very nervous about the situation. After all, how did Grandad suggest the idea to him? 'By the way, do you fancy raping my granddaughter?' How does a reputable man bring that up in conversation? It still boggles my brain to this day. His friend obviously felt uneasy, as if it might be a set-up. Now, seeing Grandad start to rape me on the sofa, he relaxed. Unzipping his fusty grey trousers, he began to masturbate. Usually my fear levels were eleven out of ten. Now they were off the scale.

As Grandad raped me, he kept turning round to the man and commenting, as if he was educating him, saying, 'This is how it's done, see what a big girl she is.' It was like a sick school for paedophiles.

But bad as this was, I knew it would get worse. There was no way this guy would just watch. I knew, at some point, he would want to join in.

Suddenly Grandad told him, 'Your go!'

The man walked over in silence, and began raping me. I was crying and crying and crying until my head throbbed in agony.

I felt a strange sense of betrayal. Grandad had always made out that I belonged to him, that I was his 'special little girl'. But I now realized that he treated me like a possession that he could pass around or give away.

Then they both raped me together, swapping every five minutes into another horrific configuration: vaginally and orally, then, finally, vaginally and anally, simultaneously. The room was silent by now, other than my screams. I was howling with pain and fear, begging them to stop, pleading for mercy.

I felt like a cat trapped in a box with nowhere to go. These two large men, heavy with their beer bellies, crushing down on me, grinding into me.

Let it be over. Let it be over. Let it be over. Let it be over. The words went through my mind with mechanical repetition.

In the past I'd worried Grandad would choke me to death. Now I wanted to die. The pain was excruciatingly bad, and death seemed my best option. It was the quickest way out. Eventually I started to lapse in and out of consciousness, one minute I felt faint, the next minute I wasn't there, then I would come round again, still trapped in the most terrifying ordeal imaginable. Once again, I would close my eyes and pray for death.

I'd perfected the art of detachment in previous ordeals, but this was too awful. I couldn't detach myself. Usually a little trap door would open up in my head and allow me to escape the physical pain into a fantasy land separate from the grim reality of my life. I desperately tried to reach that place, but the pain was so bad I couldn't. I was too young to know how to kill myself. But if someone had passed me poison, I would have drunk it. If someone had put a gun to my head, I would have pulled the trigger. I couldn't split my personality into two, and both sides converged into one me as I was ripped to pieces, trapped there like an animal.

Then it was over. I couldn't say how long it had lasted.

The atmosphere in the room was charged – with excitement for them, and with absolute sickness and fear for me.

Grandad broke the silence first. 'Pick up your clothes and clean yourself up,' he told me. There wasn't a flicker of emotion in his voice.

I ran upstairs naked and locked myself in the bathroom. Downstairs I could hear them mumbling. I didn't care what they were saying. I wanted to escape. I didn't want to go to a children's home, and I didn't want to go to jail. I wanted to die – I just didn't know how to do it.

Shivering with convulsions of fear, I gingerly inspected my battered body. I was bleeding everywhere. There were cuts, sores and bruises all over my body. The sides of my mouth were ripped, as though a blade had formed a Chelsea smile, from where they'd forced me into oral sex. It looked like I had stepped out of a car crash and had barely escaped with my life. Pain washed over me in great waves, almost knocking me off my feet.

Then Grandad banged on the door. I cowered against the wall, before opening the door a fraction, terrified they were about to attack me again.

'Drink this!' he ordered, passing me a glass full of gin.

He didn't mean for me to sip it, he wanted it knocked back in one. I gagged as he kept pushing the bottom of the glass to force it down, the sharpness of the alcohol stinging the cuts in my mouth. I don't know whether he wanted to numb my pain or try and get me drunk to confuse my memories.

Crying silently, the kind of tears that aren't for show or to get sympathy but that well up from a dark place of despair inside, I took the scrubbing brush, and tried to remove any trace of the two men from me. Blood from the ordeal mingled with blood from the scrubbing, but I didn't care. I would have ripped my skin off piece by piece if I could have.

Crawling into bed, I was like a wounded animal trying to find a safe place to pass away. I'd soaked a towel in hot water and put it between my legs, trying to relieve the pain. When I coughed it was agony. The weight of the two men bearing down on me had crushed my ribs, bruising them all over. I curled up in a ball, cuddling my rag doll, and cried myself into a shallow restless sleep, twitching with terror and pain through the night.

Next morning I woke to the smell of eggs cooking. It was a warm, homely smell. Gran was making breakfast, in what to me was a disturbing facade of normal family life. I felt I'd slipped back into a fake twilight of pretence. But when you've been through that much pain you can't forget it. There wasn't one part of me that didn't hurt the next day – I'd even hurt my toes by clenching them in pain and fear. I told Gran I'd got a sore tummy, and she assumed I'd got my period. When I shuffled to the toilet she could see I was bent double in agony. 'Poor lamb,' she told me kindly, never guessing the horrific truth of what had happened.

In bed, my mind raced with a million terrifying visions. I knew Grandad had crossed a line by taking the abuse outside his little bubble. There was no way of knowing or predicting what would happen next. From that point on I was a shell. Another part of me had died that night. Now it felt there was nothing left of me to take.

The phrase that had tormented me for so long changed. It was no longer 'What next?' It was '*Who* next?'

The thought drove me half mad with fear.

13. I'll Kill You

My life already felt like a horror movie. Now it felt like the grizzly climax was coming, where the victim fights for her life. Grandad's friend would pop round, often when Gran was at home. She'd brew him a cuppa and chatter happily about local gossip. I'd hide on the stairs and listen in on their conversation. Everything felt surreal. I'd separated my life into two worlds, but now they were overlapping. The dark side kept creeping in.

Visions of the attack haunted me when I closed my eyes at night, and flashbacks would paralyse me with fearful visitations in broad daylight.

Crouching on the stairs, I daren't get too close to the door, so I couldn't make out what they were saying. But in my heightened paranoia, I imagined they were talking about sending me away to jail or arranging for another man to attack me. The thought that he was in the house made me feel sick.

Is Gran in on it too? I'd worry to myself, trying to blink back the tears of anxiety and betrayal. Of course she wasn't, but everything was so mixed up, I believed anything was possible. Life had taught me one lesson: don't trust *anyone*. And Grandad stirred all these fearful emotions up with manipulation and threats. His cruelty was obscene.

Since the attack by the two men, rage had begun to rise

up in me. The experience had been so bad that the tricks he used to control me didn't work as well any more. By now, I didn't really care if I was sent away. How much worse could life somewhere else get? I'd think bitterly.

But one day he called me on it. I'd barely walked through the door when he pushed me forcefully over the kitchen table, trying to pull my school uniform off, so he could rape me there and then. I wriggled out from under him and in a moment of anger screamed, 'I'm going to tell Dad!'

He went white. We stared at each other for what seemed like an eternity. He was working out if I was serious. I'd meant it when I said it, but now I started to lose my nerve. Maybe he saw the look of doubt pass over my eyes.

'Right, I'll call your dad then,' he double-bluffed me. It was the counter-intuitive trick he always used on me, and once again, it threw me.

That small part of me that thought maybe Grandad was in the wrong, disappeared upon seeing his lack of concern for anyone finding out.

Am *I* going to get in trouble? I thought to myself, feeling faint.

I felt utterly powerless. I'd thrown my last piece of ammunition at him, that I'd tell, and it hadn't worked. What else could I do?

Pushing past him, I sprinted upstairs and slammed the door. Inside, I somehow found a superhuman strength to shift the wardrobe to barricade myself in. Then I sat on the floor with my back against the bed, and my legs stretched out, my feet pressing against the wardrobe to wedge it in even tighter, in case he decided to force his way in. I was shaking with terror, but the adrenalin coursing round my body tapped into my reserves of strength.

Clunking up the stairs, he started battering his fists against the door. I could hear the sound of his rasping, out-of-breath pants. He'd belted up the stairs behind me, but his age and smoking counted against him.

'Am I phoning your dad or not? It's your decision,' he screamed through the door, still hitting the wood hard with his fist.

I knew the power of that punch, and every time it cracked against the wood, I flinched in anticipated fear. Then he was quiet. What is he up to? I thought, trembling. I knew he wouldn't just give up. Within seconds my sixth sense told me. I slowly lifted my head up. He was staring intently at me through the glass partition above the door. His face had a half-demented expression of rage and barely contained violence etched across it.

Without thinking, I opened the wardrobe door and climbed in. The musky, woody warmth felt dark and safe. With my body weight pressed against the door, I felt sure he wouldn't push his way in – and he couldn't see me either.

I could hear him screaming like a madman outside, repeating his threat to call my dad. With my heart pounding, I felt my lower lip tremble. My rebellious rage dissolved into tears of fear and confusion. Dad wouldn't believe me – he'd think I was a liar and a troublemaker. The whole family already thought I was an oddball who made things up. Dad would *hate* me. I couldn't bear for him to send me away. Suddenly the weight of all those years of manipulation crushed into my mind. I opened the wardrobe door slowly, and in a small voice said, 'Don't call.'

Later that night, half feverish with fear, anguish and a swirl of doubts racing around my head, I penned my mum a letter in my still childish swirl. 'I'm sorry you don't love me,' I wrote, tears smudging the black ink. 'I'm in trouble with Grandad. I'm sorry I've been bad. I promise I'll be a good girl.'

I was too distraught to even wonder if she'd know what I was talking about.

When she received it she presumed I'd been playing up and had got a telling off and rang me to see if I was okay. I was still too scared of Grandad's threats to confess what was happening, so I reassured her I was fine.

Years later, after the truth came out, she dug the note out. In hindsight, she could see it was a desperate cry for help. For years, she carried it around in her purse, as a terrible memento of the guilt she felt. But at the time, no one had a clue what was really happening to me.

Grandad felt strengthened by the victory. His threats became even more vile. He didn't bother saying I'd be sent away any more. Instead, he liked to gloat that he was going to introduce me to even more men, and that large groups would take their turn with me. I absolutely believed what he was saying. After all, his threats always came true. I was *terrified*.

The pain had been almost impossible to bear, if there were more men I knew it would be the end of me, physically and emotionally.

Grandad also liked to taunt me that he was going to do the same thing to other girls. When his threats against me didn't work, and I fought back, he'd change tack. 'Don't then, I'll just do it to another little girl.' That thought made me feel sick. I didn't want anyone else to go through what I had. I was already violated, so I thought it better to sacrifice myself. Then, one day, he made his worst threat yet. Fighting him off, I screamed that I didn't want him to touch me. He snarled at me, narrowed his eyes and said, 'If you don't, when your mum comes up, I'm going to use the chloroform on her and rape her.'

Stunned, I stared at him for a second, then I stopped fighting back. How could he threaten my mum like that? I sobbed, saying I didn't want him to hurt her. Even though I didn't see her often, she was still my mum. The thought of her being drugged and raped destroyed me. He was beyond evil.

This battle between us raged on until I turned fourteen. I'd fight back, fuelled with anger, only to be cut down by an increasingly shocking threat or manipulation, always frightened of what he might do. Fortunately, he never delivered on his promise to gang rape me again.

Then something happened that Grandad had always predicted. However, he'd never realized it would be the beginning of the end for him. I finally started to grow up. Not his fake, perverted grown up, wearing adult lingerie, but the way a little girl starts to become a woman in her teenage years: I got my first boyfriend.

He was called Sam, and he readily admitted that he was

a virgin. I lied that I was too. I *was* a virgin in a certain sense of the word. I'd never consented to have sex. His purity and innocence made me feel safe. Sadly, I had to fake the kind of innocence that came naturally to Sam. We walked by the sea, held hands and kissed with awkward teenage passion. One night in his bedroom, observed watchfully by posters of Pamela Anderson, he gave me a small cat ornament holding a heart, and told me he loved me. Then he blushed beetroot red. I felt dizzy with emotion. Sam lived on Grandad's estate, and belonged to a crowd of kids who hung around in the evenings. We'd been introduced, and hit it off immediately. He looked like a young Patrick Swayze – I was a big fan of *Dirty Dancing* – and I couldn't believe he could like me so much. Grandad had totally destroyed my self-esteem. That night, under the snuggly warmth of his boyish duvet we both lost our virginity – his physically, mine emotionally. At the time I just melted into a warm feeling I had never experienced before, which felt confusingly nice.

When I raced home, straightening my clothes, I started to think about what had just happened. Grandad was peering through the window, looking at his watch and waiting. 'You've been with that boy, haven't you?' he said accusingly as I stepped through the door. Guilt was written across my face.

I expected him to give me a lecture, or ban me from seeing him. Instead, so Gran couldn't hear, he whispered maliciously in my ear. 'Bring him round tomorrow when your gran's out. I'll watch you both having sex through the glass over your bedroom door.' He chuckled to himself, pleased with the disgustingness of his suggestion. I pushed past him and stomped upstairs.

'What's wrong with her?' I could hear Gran ask. She thought I was becoming a horrible moody teenager and was losing patience with me.

In bed, I replayed my time with Sam over and over in my mind. I was used to terrifying flashbacks, not memories I enjoyed revisiting. It felt good. It was empowering to have said 'Yes' during sex. I'd started wearing tight jeans and stuffing my small bra with tissue paper to pad it out. A faint glimmer of sexual power had ignited in me. On the one hand, it was exciting, but it also stirred up some very dark feelings. The more I thought about it, the more confused I became. How could something so vile become something nice? I tormented myself, thinking about how one person's touch could be so different from another person's. But it also gave me something to compare it with. I started to realize with shock, that what Grandad did wasn't what normal grown-ups did. For the first time I really questioned his lies. But then, the shadows would kick in. I felt I'd asked for sexual intimacy, I'd *wanted* it. That made me feel guilty, because for years I'd associated sex with the disgusting things Grandad had done to me.

Over the next few weeks I was in turmoil. Some nights enduring vile rapes, where I begged and pleaded for Grandad to stop; other nights, applying clumsy make-up and blow-drying my long blonde hair so I would look nice for a date with Sam. Finally, this maelstrom of emotion simmered over into a crisis point. All the hatred, anger and fear had distilled into a cold, white rage against

Grandad. I was now starting to realize, beyond all doubt, that what he was doing to me was *wrong*, and not one bit normal.

The day everything blew up, I was making myself a cheese sandwich in the kitchen. I couldn't find a small knife, so I was cutting slices with one of Gran's big carving knives. I'd just got in from school, and was still in my uniform, humming away to myself, admiring my new pink nail polish as I prepared my snack. 'Oh, Mickey, you're so fine,' I sung to myself with a silly smile playing on my lips. I was thinking of Sam.

Suddenly I felt a blow to my back as Grandad bent me over the counter, his fetid tobacco breath hot on the back of my neck. He pushed my skirt up, about to rape me, mumbling dirty words in my ear.

A feeling of heat rushed over me, a powerful, instinc-tual anger. I was taller now, and in the force of my rage, I could challenge him. Clutching the knife, I whirled round and slashed it towards him.

'Come near me again and I'll KILL YOU!' I screamed, hysteria rising in my voice. The knife was shaking in my hand, but there was a look of dark determination in my eyes. Backing off, he looked genuinely frightened.

'Okay, okay,' he said, stumbling as he edged out of the room.

I carried on clutching the knife, then slowly placed it on the side, running up to my bedroom with my heart pounding.

Finally, something had snapped.

Over the next week we never mentioned the incident,

but something had changed in his attitude towards me. There was a sense of caution and restraint that had never been there before. We prowled around each other, like two defensive animals, living off our nerves. Gran sensed the tension, and put it down to my 'difficult' teenage years. I felt I was walking on the precipice of a new future. I wasn't sure whether I was about to soar away to freedom or plunge to my death.

Since I'd moved to Grandad's I had spent hardly any time at the police house. The whole point had been to separate Joan and me, so it didn't make sense for me to hang around there, getting under her feet.

This morning though, Grandad drove me down to spend the day there. We didn't speak in the car, and I put my headphones on, deliberately switching the volume up to full blast. Grandad's face was rigid, like a mask. He dropped me off, and didn't even bother to come inside.

I always felt strange back at the only place I'd ever really considered home. As I opened the door I noticed a relic from my childhood. I'd decorated an old Victorian pipe with shells, sticking them on with superglue, then painting over them with vividly coloured nail varnish. It was the kind of fanciful pastime Joan had hated me for. Now, the shells had faded to a washed-out pastel colour, and I smiled bleakly, remembering the nine-year-old girl who had sat, biting her lower lip with concentration, as she stuck the shells on. Those seized moments of happiness, creating things, painting pictures and telling stories had sustained me through the hardest times. Now I was in my teens, and even though it was still a way off, I had my eye on my sixteenth birthday in a year and a half, when I could see a different route of escape. Before, the only way out had been through a trap door in my imagination, out into a fantasy world where fairies would look after me and witches would protect me. Now, my ideas of escape had changed. The older I became, the more I realized there was a world outside the life of pain Grandad had created for me. The prison he'd erected around me had been built on my childish innocence, of not knowing there was an alternative. I was tearing the walls down piece by piece as I realized there were other people, like Sam, like friends I had started to make at school, even like the policewoman who had told me 'It's bad to touch little girls' all those years ago. I could see a different way.

'Hello?' I shouted through the house, noticing that no one was home. I heard a clank from the deepest innards of the police station, and Dad suddenly appeared through the door that joined the house to the police quarters. 'Hello, love,' he greeted me warmly. But I noticed there was a worried frown on his forehead and an inscrutable look in his eye.

I soon found out why. I poured myself an orange juice, and stood at the window looking out onto the picturesque street in front, the whitewashed cottages huddled together as if they were sheltering from the sea winds.

'We need to talk,' Dad said to me, beckoning for me to sit down.

My first thought was always the same. What have I done now?

But his tone was gentle, with a softness I hadn't heard for a long time.

'You're coming back home,' he said simply, moving

his hands in an almost welcoming gesture. 'Gran and Grandad can't cope with a teenager. You're growing up, and they're getting older . . .' He trailed off.

A look of blind incomprehension crossed my face. Then I burst into tears.

'You cried when you left, and now you're crying because you're coming back,' he joked, coming over to give me a bear hug. The way he held me hinted at regret for sending me away. He was glad to have me back.

I guessed Joan wasn't so pleased, but just like she'd railroaded him into sending me away, he'd pressured her into taking me back. The crunch had come when Grandad had point blank refused to look after me any more. The only alternative would have been for me to move to England with Mum. Dad already felt as though he'd lost his youngest son, who he barely saw, so he didn't plan on losing me. At last, someone wanted to keep me, not get rid of me. It was a turning point in my life. For once, Grandad hadn't won.

My circumstances, it seemed, could always change suddenly. I was back home, and I didn't ever have to go back to Grandad's. I sat in my old room, trying to let the information sink in. It's like when you wake up from a terrible nightmare. You don't start skipping round the room with relief. Instead, you sit in the dark with your heart pounding, swamped by uneasy feelings and snatches of terrifying flashbacks. That's how it was for me.

I wasn't about to sing 'ding dong the witch is dead' about Grandad any time soon either. I'd spent years being afraid of him, and I didn't underestimate his evil.

Looking out of the window into the sky swirling with

misty clouds, I heard a noise that made my heart burst with happiness – Lassie's jovial bark. Joan had arrived back home with Lassie in tow. I pounded down the stairs and threw myself on the floor in front of my beloved dog, kissing her head, and letting my face be licked within an inch of its life. It was a touching reunion.

Joan's sour face in the background spoke volumes. She wasn't as pleased to see me home. 'Keep to your room and be tidy!' she told me in acid tones, before taking herself off into the kitchen where she didn't have to see me.

Lassie bounded up to my room, and leapt on my bed so we could talk properly. I felt grown-up, but I was still only fourteen and could regress to being a little girl at a moment's notice. 'I'm back,' I told her with tears of happiness sliding down my face. 'We've got to look after each other now.'

Then I took her out for a walk so we could revisit our old haunts. The woods made their way down to the edge of a stony beach, with the sea rising up to a shivering, silvery horizon into the distance. Lassie sniffed the contours of the beach, prodding driftwood with her paws and barking at bushes that moved in the wind. The purity of the fresh air cleared my spirit, making me feel refreshed and rejuvenated. I could feel an inner strength boiling inside me. From this moment I *knew* I was going to tell my secret.

I just didn't know where or when or to whom.

The first thing I did was to get a part-time job as a waitress. When I saw the shifts I would be doing – evenings and weekends – I laughed at the fact that I'd finally out-smarted Grandad. Of course, he didn't give up abusing me that easily. I'd hear him phoning the house, asking Dad if I could come over and visit him. 'Sorry, Dad, she's working,' I'd hear him reply. 'She's all grown up now.'

I'd almost do a little jig of glee round my room. Dad was right – I *was* growing up. I was becoming a woman. But this time it was on *my* terms, not Grandad's. It was great to hear Grandad's sick phrase used against him, blocking his evil intentions, rather than helping him put them into practice.

Receiving my first pay packet, which was about £50, was a momentous occasion for me. It was the first bit of independence I'd *ever* had.

When you've spent your whole life trapped and abused like an animal, who doesn't even have the basic rights to a pain-free life, earning your own money and the feeling of power it gives is incredible. It sounds strange, but the first thing I did was go to the shops to buy my own underwear. After years of being forced into seductive lingerie and skimpy thongs, I wanted to wear something simple and comforting. I picked out packs of plain white belly warmers. Silly girl pants, with bows and childish pictures on the front. I wanted to reclaim my purity. For years I'd been forced to use Grandad's dirty money to purchase sleazy underwear. Handing over my own heard-earned cash to buy what *I* wanted felt so empowering. These first tastes of freedom were like bliss.

At work I had to wear a waitress uniform – the traditional tight black skirt, black tights and frilly white apron. With my long hair and carefully applied make-up,

I imagined I looked quite seductive, in a precocious teen-age way. The irony was, underneath I was wearing sexless kiddies' pants that I was still slim enough to fit into. Before, I'd looked like a little girl, but worn adult underwear; now, I looked like a woman, but wore children's underwear. My life was topsy turvy and back to front. It would take a long time to straighten me out from the kinks that Grandad had forced into my outlook on the world.

After years stuck in a nightmare world of pain, my life suddenly started moving at top speed. My relationship with Sam had only really been puppy love, and as soon as I left Grandad's, we split up. But within weeks of moving to Dad's I got my first grown-up boyfriend, and fell in love.

Daniel was an unlikely knight in shining armour. He had bright ginger hair and wore steel-rimmed specs. But he was a prince to me. He had chiselled features, an athletic body and the kindest smile I'd ever seen.

We were introduced through friends, and straight away he was smitten with me. He'd come and meet me at night after I'd finished work, and we'd kiss and chat intently as he walked me home. This felt like my first real grown-up relationship. Unlike with Sam, sex was an issue. Back then we'd been two kids fumbling around, and his absolute innocence had shielded me from the worst of my own dark, complicated emotions on that subject. With Daniel, I felt more reticent, knowing that when I crossed that line, we would embark on a proper adult relationship, and that scared me.

But he was an absolute angel. His patience and

tenderness with me melted my heart. It was as if he knew it was a place he couldn't push me towards before I was ready. It did stir up some very mixed feelings about Grandad though. I might have escaped his clutches physically, but the mental hold he had over me was like tentacles that could still strangulate me.

Part of me couldn't understand why Daniel didn't want to have sex with me. It was the same with the guys at work. Sure, they flirted with me, but they never tried it on. Instead, they became my friends, flattering me, bantering and making me laugh with silly jokes. Among all these decent men, I found I was treated with something absolutely alien to me: respect.

But as my belief in myself grew, it was as though a light had switched on in the dark room of my childhood. I suddenly saw all the misery and anguish for what it was. Not something I deserved, but something that had been forced on me by someone totally evil, who had violated my trust.

But one night, the devil of my nightmares came back for one last visit.

It was a family party at the police house, and I arrived late, at around nine, after finishing my waitressing shift. I'd called Daniel to tell him I couldn't see him that night. He took the tremor in my voice as disappointment we couldn't meet, but it was far more than that: Grandad would be there.

I steeled myself, telling the anxious voice in my head that everything would be okay, that there would be dozens of people around and he couldn't hurt me. I knew that was logical, but even the thought of breathing the same air as him made me physically sick. But what could I do? I still didn't feel able or ready to tell my secret, and Dad would wonder why I wasn't at the party.

When I walked through the door, a wall of noisy chatter hit me. The room was boiling hot, as people mingled, eating and knocking back drinks.

'Hey, the waitress has arrived!' a relative joked as I stepped into the room, dressed in my full waitress uniform.

I laughed and picked up a tray, handing round drinks. Everyone greeted me with cheers as I shimmied round the room topping up drinks and plates. It was a good way to avoid speaking properly to anyone.

But then Dad grabbed me. He turned me round, and right there in front of me was Grandad on the sofa with Gran, primly sipping on her sherry.

'Why don't you show them your new room?' he asked, his cheeks throbbing with the rosy glow of alcohol. Since I'd got back home, Dad had assuaged his guilt by giving my room a total makeover. He'd installed satellite television, a pay phone so I could make private calls, a small sofa and a big double bed. The psychedelic zigzags on the walls had been replaced by magnolia paint and a tasteful pink border. I loved it. Dad was proud of it; it was his way of trying to show *his* dad that I was okay, that finally he was looking after his daughter the way he should be.

'I'll take a look,' said Grandad straight away, his eyes glinting.

'I'll go up later,' said Gran. She'd need more incentive than teenage interior decor to walk up the narrow spiral staircase that led to my room.

I stood like a rabbit in the headlights, not knowing what to do.

Dad took my tray off me, and pushed me to the stairs.

The chatter in the room took on a hysterical tinge, and everything went momentarily out of synch. He won't hurt you, I told myself bravely.

As I walked up each step, I could feel his eyes boring into me. The waitress outfit I loved so much suddenly made me feel very uncomfortable.

Inside he nodded appreciatively, commenting on all the new furniture.

'I see you got a double bed,' he said. 'That'll be good for when you have lads stay over.' Something sinister flickered in his eyes.

Before I knew it, he had pushed me roughly over the bed, so my face was pressed into my new cream duvet, muffling any noise I tried to make.

He can't do this, he can't do this, he can't do this! My mind swam with disbelief. His own wife and son were only seconds away downstairs.

'Shut up!' he whispered fiercely into my ear. That familiar smell of tobacco, aftershave and sweat made me gag. It didn't last long, but for me it was an eternity. His sheer audacity stunned me. Wasn't I safe *anywhere*?

Afterwards, he told me to wait five minutes before I came down.

I looked at my feet, and the childish pants I had bought were in a torn heap round my ankles, but I didn't cry, or answer him back.

It was as if I had turned into a machine, which was programmed for one thing only: anger. A sentence formed in my head with such force it was as if it had kicked its way through the dark recesses of my conscious-ness.

With the sound of the festivities going on downstairs, I sat in the darkness of my room and said out loud, like a vow of vengeance: 'This will be the last time.'

14. Has He Hurt You?

On the surface my life looked perfect. I'd grown into an attractive young woman; I had a boyfriend who adored me, and a dad who spoilt me rotten.

But appearances are very deceptive. The more the mask I wore for the outside world became idealized, the more mixed up my inner emotions became. I could feel myself becoming a strong, independent woman – but this only served to highlight the terrified little girl still cowering in my subconscious.

Everyone noticed how strangely I was behaving. 'I know something's wrong,' Dad would say to me in desperation, coaxing me to talk to him. But I'd just look at him mysteriously and say, 'If I told you it would tear the family apart.' He never pressed me further. People assumed the problem was Joan. It didn't take a genius to see how much we hated each other. When I dropped hints like this, people imagined I was avoiding a family showdown with my stepmum. They guessed wrong.

This final rape sent me over the edge. The once place I'd always been safe was at the police house and now something inside me snapped.

Daniel knew I was upset, but he didn't know why. Our relationship had always been very loving – but now I couldn't even bear him to kiss me.

A week after the attack, I went to the local store and

bought a litre bottle of vodka. The sun was hanging low in the sky, spreading a rosy glow through the clouds. I headed for the beach, finding a sheltered spot where I could look across the bay, and watch the day fade away into the darkness of night.

I felt everything and nothing, all at the same time. Fear, pain, raging anger – a swirl of emotions consumed me – while a terrible numbness was spreading over me, like a slow anaesthesia, which scared me.

My plan was to get really, really drunk. I wanted to blot everything out.

I'd scrubbed myself raw in the past to cope with what had happened to me, now I wanted to drink myself into oblivion. I swigged on the bottle, gasping at the sharpness of the alcohol. After ten minutes, the edges of the world softened, and sad tears formed in the corners of my eyes. There was a pay phone on the road behind me and I decided to call Daniel. I just needed to hear his voice. I'd never felt so alone or lost in my life.

'I don't care about anything any more,' I sobbed into the phone.

'Stay right where you are, I'm coming to get you!' he replied, his voice firm, traced with the tightness of anxiety.

Half an hour later, with his arm round my shoulders, we sat and watched the shimmering water get sucked into the gloom of twilight. The wind had picked up, howling through the trees in the nearby forest, and whipping around our ears. We snuggled into each other for warmth.

'I know something's wrong; you have to tell me what it is,' he said softly.

I took another large swig from the bottle, and remained silent.

'I wish you would trust me,' he continued, sadness in his voice.

'Everyone who I trust hurts me,' I blurted out, fighting back the tears.

'But you have to trust *somebody*. No one can cope with things all on their own. I knew someone who was sexually abused, she kept silent and it didn't help her. She needed to share it with someone . . .' his words trailed off in the wind, and in the fading light he couldn't see the expression on my face. 'I'm not going to be angry, whatever it is.'

'It's my grandad.' I just said it, straight out, then gulped on the vodka for courage. The alcohol was loosening my tongue and I couldn't stop myself. I was scared of what I was saying, but also liberated. 'He's not that nice. Everyone thinks he is, but he isn't . . .' I let that thought hang in the air, waiting to be harnessed.

'Has he hurt you?'

I couldn't reply. As always, the words wouldn't form. I needed *him* to say them. There was a moment's pause.

'Has he *touched* you?' his voice rose at the end of the sentence.

I broke down crying, and from between my hands, muttered a muffled, 'Yes'.

'When was the last time?'

I hesitated, then replied, 'Last week.'

His face went bright red, as if he was about to explode with anger. 'I'm not mad at you,' he reassured me, stroking a strand of hair from my face, 'but you *have* to tell someone. I'm giving you a week to do it. Otherwise I'm going down to the police station to tell your dad myself.'

That night I lay in bed wide awake until the first light of the sun streaked the sky. I felt partly terrified and partly relieved. Whatever way, the secret was about to come out. It had festered inside me for all these years, but soon it would surface. But the consequences still terrified me. I was convinced that no one would believe me. Dad would dismiss me as a liar and hate me, I was sure. I desperately wanted to tell him. But how? I was grown up enough to know by now that what Grandad had done *was* wrong. So I realized that one of us would be sent away. If no one believed me, I'd be sent away, and if people *did* believe me, Grandad would be taken away. Either option meant breaking Dad's heart. He was about to lose a daughter or a father.

A week later, Dad had a gathering at the house with all his friends. Tom, my older brother, who was now in the armed forces, had come back home on a few weeks' leave. As always, having him near made me so happy, but he was worried about me. Dad had told him how strangely I was behaving, and had pleaded with him to try and get it out of me.

So, as the men hung around downstairs, Tom clanked his way up the spiral staircase to have a heart to heart with me. Sitting on the bed, with my school folders scattered all round me, I was catching up on my homework.

'All right, sis, what's up?' he boomed, his broad face breaking into a grin.

'All right, bro!' I replied, leaping up to hug him.

'Can I talk to you for a minute?' he said, his face becoming serious.

I sat back on the bed and folded myself into a cross-legged position, with my arms crossed defensively against my chest. He sat down beside me, his large legs crumpling the duvet.

'Dad's asked me to have a word with you,' he told me, getting straight to the point.

My heart thumped harder and harder against my chest. This is it, I told myself swallowing down the fear and panic.

'Everyone's worried about you. I know Dad's asked you before, but you've got to tell me what's wrong. Your life is great, but you're never happy. It doesn't make sense.'

I opened my mouth to respond, but before I could make an excuse, Tom interrupted me, saying, 'There's no point saying "it could break up the family". You need to tell me what's wrong.'

I remained silent, playing with my hair nervously. I'd totally seized up.

'What's wrong?'

He kept saying it with a rhythmic insistence, which started to break my already frayed defences down.

'Has someone hurt you?' he questioned me, staring intently into my face.

I nodded. It felt like the stop cap had released a massive force of pressure. I'd admitted *something* was wrong. It was only a matter of time before my brother got it out of me. He knew how to press my buttons.

'Who? Dad?'

I sat there mute, shaking my head.

'Joan?' His intonation suggested he'd hit the nail on the head.

Once again, I shook my head. This momentarily stunned him. He'd not reckoned on having her eliminated from the role call. Growing increasingly puzzled, he started to list everyone we knew – friends, family, distant relatives – until finally he said, with absolute incredulity, 'Grandad?'

It was as if he were the last person he expected to be accused.

At the mention of his name I felt every drop of life drain from my body. I nodded a barely perceptible yes.

Our eyes met, and Tom went sheet white.

'Has he hurt you?'

I nodded again.

'Has he hit you?'

I moved my head in agreement, looking at the floor.

Tom stumbled over the next words, as if they cost him a great effort to say, 'Has he touched you in places he shouldn't have?'

I started crying, clutching the edge of the bed to steady myself.

The game was up. It hadn't been a conscious decision, it was as if all those 'yes' answers had finally broken my ability to lie and say 'no'.

A pained groan came from Tom, like he'd just taken a bullet.

'Just the once?' His eyes glittered as he tried to establish how bad it was.

'Lots of times,' I confessed, between sobs, 'as far back as I can remember.'

I watched several emotions wash over his face, transforming his expression with mercurial speed – first the blankness of shock, then a wash of sickly nausea, finally brewing into boiling anger. Then it was as if a shutter came down over his face. When he opened his eyes again, he wasn't the same person, and the world wasn't the same place. He adored Grandad; he was his hero. That image shattered in front of his very eyes, and I watched it dawn on him that we'd all been living with a monster, but only I had known it.

If felt as if time was suspended. I could see he was angry – but was he angry with me? Was this the start of everyone turning against me?

I broke the moment, suddenly grabbing his hand and begging him not to tell anyone. 'Please, promise, please promise not to tell!' I pleaded.

'One thing – did that guy all those years ago touch you, like Ally said?'

'Yes,' I admitted nervously.

He clenched his hands, moaning, 'No.' Then he spun round and headed for the stairs. 'Wait here,' he told me. Our eyes met again. His were full of compassion and love for me – mixed with the horror and confusion at what our grandad had done. Mine were blank with sheer terror. As soon as he left, the panic hit me. I *knew* he would tell Dad.

I grabbed my school bag and emptied the contents onto the bed, then stuffed whatever clothes I could find from my drawers in it. I had to escape. Looking round frantically, I couldn't see a way out. If I went down the stairs Dad would see me. I glanced at the window. I couldn't, could I? It was a long drop down. But by now I was half crazy with fear.

'Emily!' my dad's authoritative voice brought me back to my senses. I'd got one leg out of the window, about to jump.

'Sorry,' mouthed Tom, as he stepped to the side so Dad could come forward into the room, 'I had to do it.'

Dad's face was contorted with pain. Shock had twisted his features into an open wound of conflicting emotions.

We stared at each other. It was a life-changing moment.

Would he believe me? It was as though he had a gun, and was about to play Russian roulette with his answer.

'I believe you,' his voice broke into an anguished croak as he spoke.

Like a rabbit in the headlights, I didn't know what to do next. Suddenly he rushed forward and grabbed me into a big bear hug. It was the only way he knew how to communicate all his love and sorrow. But unfortunately, he'd chosen the wrong method. The way he held my neck, harder than he realized in the intensity of the moment, reminded me of Grandad, and how he pinned me down during all those many, many rapes.

Suddenly, all the anger and frustration that had been brewing over the last few years finally unleashed in one massive torrent against my father. As he held me I kicked, fought, screamed, bit him, scratched, tearing into him – I was like an animal gone wild, totally out if its senses. Dad just stood there and took it. If the violence of my attack shocked or hurt him, he didn't show it. No doubt, in some way he felt he deserved it. He almost wanted me to punish him for all the years I'd been hurting, and he hadn't protected me.

Finally, exhausted, I collapsed into his arms, and then the tears began. He gently laid me on the bed. For a moment I felt like a young child again, before my innocence had been shattered.

'I'll get a cloth to cool your face down,' he said tenderly. The warmth coming from his eyes broke me down in tears all over again.

'Your grandad is dead to me from this day on,' he added with a fierce grimness. Then he left the room, with Tom following close behind him.

A few minutes later Joan made her way up with a damp flannel and a hot cup of tea. Stroking my forehead to soothe me, it was the first time in my life she'd ever treated me like a human being. My sobs reduced to intermittent snuffles, and I wriggled down into the duvet to feel snug and safe.

But after ten minutes, a thought suddenly dawned on me: I've just told this big secret, and no one's here. Where are they?

I turned to Joan with a questioning look on my face and asked, 'Where have they gone?'

'They've gone to find him,' she admitted, not able to meet my eyes.

I sat up in bed, scared as hell. Grandad would turn them against me. He was so manipulative, I didn't doubt for a second he would twist the truth. Everyone would think I was a liar. An uncontrollable tremor consumed my body. As soon as I'd passed one stage, there was another hurdle to go.

It was an hour until Tom and Dad got back. It was longer than a lifetime to me.

They'd gathered all the family, all the clan, to confront him. Now they walked through the front door of the police house with ravaged expressions and stooping postures. It looked like they'd just fought a war. Sitting round the fire, they explained what had happened. The kettle was permanently boiling, and someone draped a blanket over my shoulders.

My heart pounding, I tried to make sense of things, as Dad's words spilled out. It was slowly dawning on me: they still believed me.

'We drove over to his house, there were two cars of family men,' explained Dad, sitting on the edge of his chair, adrenalin still pumping round his body. 'Can you imagine answering the bell and your *entire* family being on your doorstep? He *knew* as soon as he saw us all.'

'He came to the door in a dressing gown,' Tom picked up the story. 'Dad pushed by him saying, "This isn't a social call." Grandad sat on his chair, he was shaking so much he could barely light his cigarette. Dad came straight out with it, "There's been some serious allegations, that you've been abusing Emily." Being a policeman, even the way he said it made it sound like a formal accusation.'

'What did he say?' Joan interrupted, eager to know his reaction.

'He pleaded like a coward, saying, "No, no, that's my

princess. I would never do that"—' then Tom broke off, unable to carry on.

Dad took over with a look of steely fury. 'Then he cried like a baby, saying he'd only done it the once.' A look of distaste passed over his face, as if he was swallowing a ball of guilt and hatred all at once.

'I gave him an ultimatum. I told him he's got two days to tell Mum, then we call the police.' His shoulders sagged on saying the last word. The 'police' wasn't some distant notion of law-keeping at the end of a 999 call. They were his colleagues, his friends, men who respected him. He prided himself on his ability to protect his community – especially women. He'd arrested rapists and paedophiles many times, and watched as women with broken spirits were taken by female officers for questioning and examinations.

Like most men, for him, the most despicable crime in the world was to hurt a woman – worse still, a defenceless little girl. He was trained to spot the signs of abuse in other people, but he'd missed it right under his own nose. He'd taken it for granted that his family was a place of safety. How could he have suspected his own father? The upstanding paramedic, the man who'd inspired him to join the police force, with his talk of serving the community.

Dad slumped over the table, and Joan put her arms round him for comfort.

Tom came and cuddled me. The atmosphere in the room had changed from the tension of earlier to a sombre, almost funereal feel. It was like someone had died. In a way they had. The man the family had all loved was gone. In his place was a vile pervert who deserved to rot in prison.

The rest of the day passed in a swirl of surreal talk, silence and tears. It was like being in the eye of the perfect storm. That night in bed, with Lassie nestled into the crook of my legs, I stared at the ceiling. I could hear the wind howling over the sea in the distance, and I knew, only ten minutes' drive away, Grandad would be lying in his own bed, staring at his own ceiling, feeling the kind of fear he'd usually inflicted on me. His life was no longer his own, just like my life hadn't been my own for all those years. He'd dehumanized me in the most degrading ways possible, and now he would have to pay for what he'd done. The thought gave me no comfort.

Of course, I wanted justice, but what about me? Would I get those lost years back? He could be locked up, but it would be harder to set myself free.

I was still stunned that my secret was out – and that everyone believed me.

But the white noise of Grandad's malicious manipulations still buzzed round my mind. I still didn't *feel* loved; I still didn't *feel* wanted; I still didn't *feel* free. The cocoon of loneliness and pain that had built up around me over the years would be hard to escape from. If anything, I felt more afraid than ever.

The next day was crisp and bright. The sky looked like it had been washed clean, with the clouds fluffier and whiter than ever. I had been excused from school, so I planned to walk through the cemetery and revisit my old haunts, then pace through the woods, listening to the soothing whisperings of the trees. I'd called Daniel to tell him the news, but for now, I wanted to be alone. The plaintive cry of the seagulls was company enough for me.

Dad looked sick over breakfast, like a sudden illness had devoured him overnight. I'd never seen him this defeated. 'I'm driving to Yorkshire to tell your mum,' he announced. It wasn't news that could be broken over the phone. He had to let her know in person. She didn't see much of me, but I was still her baby, and the news would break her heart.

That evening at the police house, with my hands still frozen by the hours sitting at the edge of the woods staring aimlessly out to sea, trying to make sense of my life, the phone rang. It was Mum. Dad was on his way back home, and she'd rung as soon as he'd left. 'I've let you down,' she said in a cracked voice over the phone. 'I wish you could have told me, I would have helped you. Are you all right?'

'He made threats against you,' I told her, my adult persona crumbling at the sound of my mum's comforting voice. 'He said he'd rape you too.'

I could hear her crying on the other end of the line. 'Oh baby, I can look after myself. It's you I'm worried about.'

I couldn't answer. Silent sobs wracked my body. Suddenly I remembered Mum's warm laugh, the way she'd brushed my hair with gentle strokes and the cosy nights watching telly together. A love welled up in my heart, not just for her, but for the little girl she'd left behind, and lost for ever.

The oddest feeling spread over me – it was as though I was a stranger looking in at my own life. Everything seemed to be happening at a great distance from myself. Even the fact that my mum wasn't someone real by my side, but a disembodied voice down a crackling telephone line, added to this feeling of disconnection. Something inside me was floating away, and I couldn't catch it. I was as weightless and unreal as the fairies I'd read about for so many years. The only way I knew to anchor my body down was pain. For years I'd believed that no one loved or wanted me, and that Grandad's world of pain was the only place I belonged. To realize that my parents *had* loved me, but they'd made mistakes, and that Grandad had twisted them to his own evil advantage, just took my breath away. My mind had become a series of misfiring crossed wires, with conflicting messages. I crumpled inside, and whispered, 'I love you Mum,' into the phone, before placing it back down.

Climbing into bed, it finally started to sink in: I was free.

15. Secret's Out

'I'm going to kill myself, I've taken tablets,' Grandad told Dad over the phone. The drugs he'd once used against me, he'd now turned against himself in the ultimate act of cowardice.

'You're not getting off that easy,' growled Dad, slamming the receiver down and racing over to his house.

Within an hour Grandad had been admitted to a nearby mental facility. He hadn't dared tell Gran, and he had wanted the easy way out.

Following his suicide attempt, they kept him in the hospital wing of the psychiatric unit. Dad presumed this was the best place for him to be, but a week later, he received another call, this time from a nurse at the hospital. She told him that Grandad was about to check himself out, and asked if Dad could pick him up. 'Keep him there while I drive over,' he warned her.

At the hospital he discovered that Grandad hadn't told anyone the full truth. He'd claimed to be having a mental breakdown due to family issues, and had left it at that. From the beginning, he was unable to admit what he'd done.

My father spoke to the doctors and put the record straight. He said that Grandad had been accused of raping and abusing his own granddaughter, and that he shouldn't be released from the hospital. With Dad's cooperation, the doctors called the police and alerted social workers. The police immediately launched an investigation into the allegations and, by the end of the day, Grandad had been sectioned. He was no longer free to leave the hospital.

For the moment, I was safe.

To describe the week after the confession as a whirlwind of tears, traumas and aftershocks would be an understatement. After the first impact had settled down, the family slowly but surely started to fall apart.

Gran came round to see me, and for the first time ever I could see *real* emotion in her eyes. The prim, respectable facade she put up was crumpled into regret. 'I'm sorry,' she told me, sitting ramrod straight, as if she'd been electrocuted. 'You should have told me.'

It was hard to find the words. We'd both lived in that house together, and those unspeakable things had happened under her own roof.

'I would have believed you –' She broke off, and collapsed across the table, sobbing. I'd never seen Gran emotional over *anything*. Now she was an emotional mess. It was frightening to see such an uptight woman lose control like that. No doubt she felt she'd lost everything.

Dad was leaning on the oak table as if the weight of what had happened was too much to bear. His expression was that of a man in torment. The police force had already signed him off on immediate sick leave. 'How can I look after other people when I can't look after my own family?' I'd heard him mutter down the phone. His colleagues supported him, but they couldn't take away his guilt and shame. He had to come to terms with it on his own. Along with the horror of finding out what had happened to his little girl, he was also dealing with the loss of his father, and now his mother was breaking down before his eyes.

His entire world was falling apart.

Ending my silence had changed me too. It was as if a fiercely angry person had been unleashed from a box and set loose. The violence of the emotions I had repressed all those years was set free. I couldn't control my temper. It wasn't a conscious decision, but the smallest thing could set me off. I reacted badly to everything. I'd spent so many years forced to be 'Grandad's good little girl' and now I was lashing out.

Dad was unravelling at a rapid rate too. Every time he saw me, he was raw with emotion. It was as if, by looking at me, he was constantly reminded of what Grandad had done. It absolutely killed him. He just couldn't cope.

But not surprisingly, I wasn't in a mood to be sympathetic.

What about me? The thought raced round my mind like an angry rant. I'd been nothing before, now I wanted my feelings to count.

A week later everything came to a head. I'd been suspended from school due to my angry erratic behaviour. The news was too much for Dad. All the unspoken grudges, guilt, betrayals boiled over into a massive row. The trauma hadn't bonded us together – it had torn us both apart.

'It's best if you go and stay with Mum,' Tom told me

the following morning, 'just for a couple of days until things calm down.'

I called Daniel and told him the news, promising him I'd be back in a few days. He was my lifeline, and I didn't know how I'd cope without him, but I knew I couldn't stay at the police house for the moment. The atmosphere was too explosive. My father and I needed a break from each other.

'I love you Emily,' Mum threw her arms round me, uttering those words that for the first time since Grandad had poisoned my mind, I could start to believe. 'I love you too,' I cried, collapsing into her arms.

Mum felt guilty too, but things between us weren't as complicated as between Dad and me. It was a relief to finally let her hold me in her arms. I felt like the little girl I'd been before I'd lost myself to Grandad.

Mum hadn't changed over the years; she was still the immaculately turned out lady she had always been. The house was beautifully furnished in soft shades of pastel, it was warm and inviting, like something from the pages of a homes and lifestyle magazine.

But being with her couldn't fix my problems. I felt strangely off kilter, like a stranger in my own life. I didn't feel I belonged anywhere.

As we sat opposite each other, on separate couches, clutching cups of tea, we started to talk – to *really* talk for once. Mum explained how heartbroken she'd been when I'd chosen to stay in Scotland, and not come with her. I told her what Grandad had told me – how I believed she would send me to an orphanage. She shook her head with sadness and disbelief. Her perfectly manicured nails tapped on the side of the china teacup with pent-up anxiety.

'That man disgusts me,' she almost hissed. 'I'm still in shock. You do know he's the one in the wrong, don't you?' I'd already told her how I'd believed it was my fault all these years, and that's why I'd kept silent. She was determined to make me realize that I was the innocent one in all this. Tentatively, she started to question me about the abuse. Up until now, we'd only euphemistically talked about Grandad 'touching' me. It had been too sensitive a subject to go into details. But Mum was ready to broach the subject – even though I wasn't.

'Did it stop at touching?' she asked. 'God knows that's bad enough, but I need to know if that beast went further –'

I jumped out of the chair screaming, 'Don't ask me that! Don't you dare!' My emotions were like a hair trigger, they could flip into hysteria at the slightest suggestion. Since I'd told my secret, my family had fallen apart. If I admitted he'd raped me – and worse – I worried what else would happen. It seemed the more I told, the worse things got.

Mum's face became still with an unspoken knowing. 'Judging by that reaction, I've got my answer.'

She didn't come over to comfort me. With a woman's intuition, she knew that at this moment I didn't want to be touched.

A few moments later, she walked into the hall and picked up the phone. 'Could I speak to the chief inspector?' I could hear her say. Then silence. 'No, it's much worse than we thought. I want things to move quickly, these are very serious allegations.'

The police were already investigating the matter, but at Mum's instigation they fast-tracked the case. The problem was, with me in Yorkshire and Grandad in Scotland, there were two different police jurisdictions involved and this complicated matters. Mum made it clear that she didn't want red tape to stop justice being done. Grandad needed to be punished for his crime.

She had also put her foot down about something else. 'I lied, you're not going home in a few days, you're staying with me now. You need your mum at a time like this,' she told me in a no-nonsense tone.

'You can't keep me here, I want to go back home. I need to see Daniel!' I flew at her shouting a torrent of abuse. 'I'm going to run away. I hate you. When I'm sixteen I'm leaving – and you can't stop me!'

I was irrational and out of control, but Mum let me rant on and never retaliated. She felt she'd let me down before and now she was determined to be there for me – even if I didn't want her to be. I was too confused to know *what* I wanted. But I was sure of one thing. I wanted to make my own decisions. After Grandad, I never wanted anyone to have control over me again. Not even my mum. I felt I was being held against my will.

I crawled into bed, full of rage. How long would I feel like a caged animal trapped in my own life? Mum's house only had two bedrooms, and the two boys – my two younger brothers – shared a bunk bed. Now they were curled up in the bottom bunk, and I was stranded in the top one.

I slept fitfully that night, waking up to giggles and prods from mischievous young boys, too young to understand what their older sister was going through. 'Leave me alone!' I roared at them. They looked at me like I was a madwoman, and I turned over, trying not to snap at them again.

A week later Mum drove me to a specialist child protection unit to be interviewed by the police. This was the first time I had made an official statement about the abuse, and I was *terrified*. It felt as though I was cutting through invisible cords still linking me to Grandad's threats. Talking to the police brought all those old, irrational fears back, Would I be thrown in the police cell? Was this all an elaborate trick? I chewed my fingernails anxiously, as Mum focused on the road, her jaw clenched tight.

The unit looked like a living room, with a battered couch in the centre. A friendly-looking policewoman greeted me, and her colleague, another homely looking woman, stood behind her. They weren't in uniform, and that settled my nerves slightly. My social worker, a cheery woman with round glasses, was also present, and waved hello with a slightly strained smile. Everyone knew this wasn't going to be easy for me.

'Now don't be nervous, but there'll be cameras pointed at you,' one of the policewomen told me as she led me into a separate room. Contrasted with the plain white walls and plastic table and chairs, the two black cameras in each corner, staring down, appeared to dominate the room. It was like asking someone walking a tightrope not to look down. Instinct makes you do it. I felt the lenses of the cameras boring into me from the moment I entered the room, and a chill went down my spine. They reminded me of Grandad's cold, calculating look, as he spied on me through the patio window and through the glass panel above my bedroom door.

Mum left me, forcing herself to let go of my hand as she was led away to watch me make my statement on the screen in an adjoining room.

As soon as the interview started, I felt myself slipping back in time from fifteen years old to six years old. The stark walls and firm voices made me regress into a child. How could I tell them what had happened? How could I put that nightmare world of pain and fear into words that could be written in a police report? I knew they only wanted the facts, but the truth was, the facts were barely adequate to explain what had happened. It was like trying to tell someone a bad dream. The memory stays with you, but it is almost impossible to get across to another person. It consists of sensations, moods, moments, the suggestions stored in the dark corners of a child's mind where words can be more powerful than handcuffs to force you against your own will. How to explain a person can rape your body, tearing your youthful flesh, while your imagination races off, chasing witches through the clouds, and fairies through the woods, how the two worlds get completely mixed up, until life becomes a dark, dark hell you can't find your way out of.

The policewomen were matter of fact. 'When did it first start? Where did he first touch you? When did he first rape you? What did he do?'

Their questions were like tiny, ineffectual drops of

water trying to join a big, black ocean of despair and suffering that spread with fathomless depths.

I pointed to my flower and my budding breasts, but I couldn't bring myself to say the words they wanted to hear. It all sounded too pornographic. These words described sexual acts, but what had happened to me hadn't been *sex* – there was no dictionary invented, no language on the earth that had the words to describe what he had done. In layman's terms, I could tell them he had made me perform oral sex on him. But didn't that put it in the context of sex and make it sound as if I was part of it in some way? It made me feel guilty and dirty to even think of it in those terms. The words couldn't stretch far enough to encompass both meanings – consensual pleasure and the violence of a degrading assault. By the time I had to try and explain how and when he'd raped me, I fell to pieces. I tried to say, in the best way I could, what had happened, in between gulps of breath and convulsions of tears. I felt ashamed and humiliated. When I told them what he'd threatened to do to Mum, I winced and looked up at the cameras. I remembered she was watching, listening to everything I said. I felt I'd tainted her by my words, and brought her into my warped world. More than anything, I wish she hadn't insisted on sitting through it. How could a mother cope with hearing a confession like that? To this day, she is still scarred by it.

When it was over. Mum and I drove home in silence. She'd heard enough, and I'd said all I could. All we could do was be there for each other.

Two days later, I went back for my medical examination. I'd got my period the day before and I begged and begged them to postpone it, but they wouldn't budge. Reports had to be filed to some official on a specific date, and the whims of my body couldn't be taken into account. Grandad needed to be formally charged, and they needed this report to nail him. Somehow, even now, concerns that related to him were greater than mine.

The examiner was a wee, dumpy woman, who looked the spitting image of Joan. Her face was stern, and she had an emotionless, clinical attitude.

'Take off your pants,' she told me, with no pleasantries. 'It'll be over soon.'

It felt as if I was being violated all over again. The police kept telling me no one could touch my body without my consent, but my experience here contradicted that. I blatantly told the examiner I didn't want to do it and I explained why. 'I'll come back in a couple of days,' I said, trying to reason that I had my period and I felt dirty down there.

She was having none of it and bullied me onto the table.

I honestly felt like I was being raped. I'd said no, but here I was being forced into letting someone touch me in the most intimate place against my will. I sobbed hysterically the whole way through while Mum held onto my hand crying herself. Afterwards I felt numb and traumatized. Even to this day, as a result of that examination, I have to be sedated to have something as simple as a smear test. It intensified the emotional turmoil I was in to an unbearable level.

Back home, I ran to my room and lay silently in bed

staring blankly at the wall, trying to switch on my default setting of numbness.

Despite my emotional agony, things went on as normal. My life felt like a frozen clock, while everyone else's was ticking along as usual. It was coming up to Christmas, but I couldn't join in with the festivities. Mum had put up a Christmas tree for the sake of my brothers, but the fairy lights would go out of focus as I stared into space, turning events over in my mind. I was still terrified of Grandad, convinced he'd come and get me. He knew where I lived. A few weeks before Christmas, a card arrived – with his name on it. Luckily, Mum had opened it as it was addressed to the entire family. But I felt his evil presence had somehow entered the house, reminding me that he could still reach me if he wanted. In reality, that wasn't the case. He was sectioned in a psychiatric hospital. But after years of threats and abuse, logic and reason didn't figure very highly. I descended into a deep depression, unable to leave the house on my own. Walking down the street was an ordeal for me. I'd have flashbacks, imagining he'd jump out and drag me into his car. I didn't want to walk round the shops and buy Christmas presents, or join in with the carol singers, going from house to house, singing happily to strangers. I wanted to hole myself away, making sure I was safe.

Then, a week after Christmas, Mum got a call. It was the chief inspector who was looking after my case. I waited nervously in the living room.

'He's been arrested, and they're not giving him bail,' Mum told me triumphantly.

'He's in jail?' I asked, barely able to believe it was true.

'Yes. He can't hurt you now, baby,' Mum replied, tears rolling down her face. I got up and hugged her, crying with relief myself.

The first thing I did was have a shower. Then I meticulously applied my make-up and put on my best outfit. I'd let myself go over the last month, hardly even bothering to brush my hair. Striding down the stairs, I flicked my hair, glanced in the mirror, and gave myself a beaming smile.

'I'm going out,' I announced to Mum, who stood by looking shocked.

'Where?' she asked, taken aback by the turnaround in my behaviour.

'Just out.' I smiled enigmatically as I walked past her.

I had no plans – I just wanted to savour my new freedom.

Walking down the street, I breathed in the cold January air with deep gasps. Finally I could breathe. He was locked away.

All these years he'd threatened I would be thrown in prison, but now he'd got his just desserts and it was him sat in a cell. I knew he had to go to trial, and that the judge might release him, but for now I was safe. Momentarily, I felt the toxic cloud that hovered over my life lifted. My eyes glittered with joy as I strode up ordinary streets, watching normal people going about their every day business, feeling part of the world again. It was a beautiful, bittersweet moment, especially because I knew it might not last.

16. Fight for Justice

The trial date was set for June. By now I had turned sixteen and had moved back to Scotland to live with Daniel and his family. During the last few months we'd spoken on the phone to each other constantly, and he'd been a big support to me. Things were still too raw between Dad and I for us to live with each other. The closer the date got, the more stressed I became. The feeling of safety started to fade with every second.

I hadn't met Grandad since I'd broken my silence – and I was terrified of seeing him in court. But I was also determined to stand up and face him finally. I wanted to confront him and say, 'I'm not scared any more.'

I wanted to take my power back. I wanted to see him with clear eyes, as a wizened old man, not the terrifying monster who had ruined my life.

The night before the case, I felt sick. I fell asleep on the sofa, too tired and emotionally exhausted to even drag myself into bed. Dad had offered to drive me to the court, but as a policeman he couldn't be present at the trial.

Instead, Mum had driven up from Yorkshire to support me.

The morning of the trial was warm and balmy. I'd awoken at the first light of day, instantly alert with the adrenalin pounding round my body. The trial began at nine thirty.

So far Grandad had pleaded not guilty to the charges against him, which meant I'd have to give evidence and be questioned in front of a jury. My barrister reassured me that there would be a screen between Grandad and me, so he couldn't intimidate me with the staring eyes that had always scared me so much. But just the thought of sharing the same air as him made me feel sick.

The courthouse was an imposing Gothic building, with reddish stonework tinged black at the edges. It reminded me of the Witch's Castle. Inside, the decor was modern and impersonal though. Mum squeezed my hand as my barrister ushered me into a meeting room with a stark white table and cheap plastic chairs.

'I'm scared I won't find the words to say what happened,' I said to her with a worried frown. I still struggled to describe what Grandad had put me through. Saying it out loud made it too real.

'Don't worry, everyone will understand if you find it hard,' she reassured me. 'Just do your best, that's all we can ask.'

I nodded, noticing that my hands felt cold and clammy, despite the heat.

As she flicked through her papers, there was a loud knock on the door. Both Mum and I started with fear. Our nerves were so frayed we reacted to every unexpected noise with a jump.

Grandad's barrister walked in. He was a self-assured, direct man and he signalled to my barrister that he wanted to talk in private. It was only five minutes before the trial was due to start. I looked at mum with a worried frown. I was only sixteen and the legal process intimidated me. Everyone explained what was happening, but they used big words and complicated terms. After what I'd been through, it was hard to get a grip on what to expect. Because of Grandad's abuse of power, I was afraid of authority. The court was a scary place that didn't feel very child friendly. With my smart blue jacket on, I suddenly felt like a little girl playing at grown-ups. Part of me didn't know whether I wanted to run away, burst into tears or curl up in a ball under the table and wait for it all to go away. Only my anger kept me fired up, giving me the strength to carry on. After all these years of keeping my silence, I wanted to stand up and tell my story. Most girls my age were spending the summer having carefree fun, looking forward to taking the first steps into the adult world, but here I was, about to face a judge and tell complete strangers how my own grandfather had robbed me of my childhood by raping and abusing me.

I felt a strange mix of a jaded weariness, alongside a childish naivety. There was still a little girl trapped inside of me, too frightened to come out.

Our barrister came back into the room with an inscrutable look on her face.

'Your grandfather's changed his plea to guilty,' she said matter of factly.

I couldn't tell if this was a good or a bad thing. Surely it was good?

'Why?' I asked, puzzled by this development. I knew he still didn't feel guilty for what he'd done, and held me responsible for ruining his life. Why would he suddenly change his mind? It didn't make sense.

'His barrister advised him he'd get a shorter sentence if he pleaded guilty. With the evidence against him, it's unlikely he'd get off.'

A bitter smile played on my lips. On one hand it was good news that he'd changed his plea – I wouldn't have to stand in front of everyone and give evidence. But even though I'd dreaded it, now that option had been taken away, I felt robbed of my moment to accuse him face to face. But worst of all, once again his actions had been disgustingly self-motivated. He hadn't wanted to spare me the ordeal of a trial – he just wanted to save his own skin. There was nothing human left in his heart.

'What happens now?' asked my mother, looking pensive. She was also struggling to keep up with the complexities of a major court case. It's such a world away from normal life, it was almost impossible to understand.

'Because he's already pleaded guilty, the trial goes straight to sentencing.' The barrister shuffled her papers efficiently and stood up. 'It's starting in a few moments, so we should really walk through.'

I tried to stand up, but my legs wobbled and I sank back into the hard plastic of the chair. Mum linked her arm with mine so I could lean on her as we entered the courtroom for the first time. The sound of our heels clomping on the hard tiled floor reverberated along the corridor, and I cringed, imagining that the sound was announcing our arrival to everyone inside.

The court was open to the public so in the upper tier nosy strangers jostled among each other to take a look at the little girl at the centre of the trial. Their prying eyes felt invasive, their presence a violation of my privacy. I felt sick with paranoia, convinced they were pointing at me, whispering, 'There's the girl who's been raped.' I was labelled as a victim and I hated it. I felt uncomfortable. I didn't want pity, or to be singled out as different. I could see members of the press among the crowds, scribbling in notebooks. They were chewing gum and nibbling on their pens, with blank expressions on their faces; for them it was just another day at work.

The high ceiling seemed to echo the noise, and for a moment I felt faint. Mum guided me along, as we inched our way along a solid wooden pew, not too different from the ones you find in church. Other family members followed us, sitting in the same row, ready to offer support if we needed it. I fiddled with my hair, trying to swallow, unable to control the sensation of extreme dryness in my throat. I felt like choking. The noise was muffled but pervasive, like the chatter in church before the priest hushes everyone for prayers. Suddenly, it went quiet. The silence was eerie, and in panic I glanced round at Mum.

'What's happening?' I whispered to her, noticing that the number of policemen present had doubled within the last few seconds.

'It's him,' she said grimly, looking straight ahead. 'It's your grandad.'

My heart fell down a lift shaft and hit the bottom at high speed.

'Where?' I asked, looking round with confusion. I couldn't see him anywhere. His face was etched on my memory, but no one fitting my mental image was in sight.

I gripped the seat in front, looking round wildly. Then I saw a pathetic-looking old man, his clothes hanging off his skinny frame. My jaw hung open. It couldn't be ... Was that really him? The last time I'd seem him, he'd been a powerful man, over six feet tall, with a beer belly that hung over his trousers. Now he was a shadow of himself and I barely recognized him.

Is that it? I thought to myself with incredulity. Is that what I've been scared of all these years? I could barely believe it. It was like seeing the little old man behind the illusion of the almighty Wizard of Oz.

Prison life hadn't been kind to him, but it was more than that. Without helpless little girls to dominate, his power had slipped away. He'd fed off my fear and, now I was in control, he was reduced to a pathetic old man.

After staring for a few seconds, I noticed the handcuffs on his wrists. A burly policeman stood on each side of him. I remembered all the times he'd pinned me down by my slim childish wrists, applying such force I'd fear they'd break. Now he was the one being restrained. It was surreal.

The judge convened the hearing, and began to read out the charges against him. It felt so invasive to have this strange man tell the court in clinical terms what had been done to *me*. I'd always found it hard to use formal words to describe the abuse, but the legal documents were very clinical in their terminology. The judge's voice turned into an oppressive drone in my head, and a rising hysteria gripped my chest like a vice. I tried to breathe from my stomach, but my lower ribcage gripped tighter and tighter.

'He inserted his penis into her vagina ...' I heard the

judge say the words impassively, and I swallowed a sob. I felt disgusting, humiliated and ashamed. Everyone knew exactly what he'd done to me and I felt dirty. I wanted to make him stop saying these things. They were *my* secrets. 'He injured my spirit not just my body!' I wanted to scream out. But those charges were indescribable and too unfathomable to read out.

The court was trying a case of sexual abuse, but what I'd suffered went far beyond that. Everything a child takes for granted as the basic right of a human being had been removed from me, piece by piece. To survive, I had somehow evacuated my own body, leaving an empty shell behind. This disconnection, this emotional numbness, was a form of murder. Grandad had killed part of me. Just like a person's soul is said to leave its body upon death, so does the spirit of a young child when being seriously abused. Finding a way back is a long torturous journey, not always guaranteed to succeed. But I wouldn't get a chance to explain this to the court. My grandfather's crimes were just read out like a shopping list of sexual offences, with no emotional context.

Mum could sense my hysteria was getting out of control as my body convulsed with sobs and trembles of distress.

'Emily I know this is hard,' she whispered, comforting me gently, 'but you have to stay strong. If you lose it, they might ask you to leave the court.'

She desperately wanted me to be there to hear the verdict. Knowing that I'd believed *I* was in the wrong for so long, she wanted me to witness with my own eyes a court of law condemn Grandad for his crimes.

With a great effort I pulled myself together, reducing my sobs to occasional sniffles. I knew I had to be here. I *needed* some form of closure.

The judge's voice was deep and compelling as he summed up in a sombre tone. 'I am disgusted by these crimes,' he boomed. 'In all my time as a judge this is by far the worst case I have ever come across.'

Following the police investigation, it turned out that Grandad's talk about abusing other girls hadn't been lies. Another eighteen victims had come forward after his arrest. I felt so confused and shocked that it had happened to so many others. As I heard the judge list the crimes committed against the other girls, my heart went out to them. But the charges on my account were by far the worst, with the longest list cataloguing Grandad's offences.

The courtroom was absolutely silent. Even the vague coughing and shuffling sounds people had been making earlier had stopped.

'Please rise for the sentencing,' the judge asked the accused.

The silence seemed to intensify in my mind. You could hear a pin drop. I was even afraid to take a breath. Time elongated, so those few seconds it took him to speak the words stretched into an eternity in my mind. Please, please, please, I begged quietly.

'I hereby sentence David Christie to twenty-seven years in jail . . .'

There was an explosion of noise, as the entire place erupted with clapping and jubilant cheers. Everyone was hugging each other, wiping tears of relief from their faces and making victory signs.

I stood in shock. It was like being in a library and then suddenly everyone going crazy. Mum looked at me, her eyes blurring with tears, then she hugged me, almost lifting me off our feet.

'We did it,' she said proudly. 'We got him!'

In the chaos we barely heard what the judge said next. Grandad had been accused of several separate crimes, relating to different things including incest, grooming and manipulation. All the charges relating to each girl had been given separate sentences, which all added up to twenty-seven years. The judge finished by saying that Grandad would serve the sentences concurrently.

We walked out, our heads held high, ready for the celebrations to start.

This wasn't just about punishing Grandad, it was about making sure other children were safe, that my future kids were safe. I couldn't take back what he'd done to me, so what counted was making sure he couldn't do it to anyone else. For this reason, I was overjoyed by the result.

The barrister met us in the corridor. Her face looked surprisingly grim. I imagined that professional people always looked this way, not wanting to let emotion overcome them. I tried to smile at her.

'Can we speak?' she asked us, showing us back into the meeting room we'd been in before. Her body language was very tense. Instantly, we felt a massive downer. We couldn't understand her attitude.

'What's wrong?' asked Mum with concern. None of us sat down.

'I don't think you quite understood the sentencing,' she said, with an apologetic inflection coming into her voice.

'He got twenty-seven years,' Mum said, taken aback, 'more than we'd hoped for.'

'But the sentences run *concurrently*,' she corrected Mum.

'What does that mean?' I butted in, confused by the jargon.

'It means that he only serves the *longest* sentence,' she explained.

'But that was only seven years,' said Mum, aghast.

'That's right. Plus he gets the six months he's spent on remand deducted, and he could get two years off for good behaviour.' She could barely meet our worried gazes as we heard this shocking news.

'But that only adds up to four and a half years.' My mother sat down as if someone had punched her.

I stood rooted to the spot, a look of confusion, shock and anger starting to ripple across my face.

'He abused me for nine years. He hasn't even got a year for every year of my life he stole,' I said in a tight little voice, my throat constricting at the realization that this *wasn't* a victory. We'd been massively let down.

Grandad had somehow beaten the system, he'd won.

Now the judge's words flooded back to me. They had been on the periphery of my consciousness because I hadn't understood their implication. He'd said something about Grandad being an old man in bad health, who had spared me the ordeal of giving evidence at trial by pleading guilty. This had counted in his favour – even though he had only done it for himself. Once again, I felt Grandad's feelings had been put before mine.

The barrister explained that it would be hard to appeal against the decision as Grandad had already pleaded guilty. It was almost impossible to change the sentencing on a guilty verdict. Nor could he be retried either.

It was as if a vacuum had sucked all the air out of the room.

The two policewomen who had worked on my case since the day I made my first statement came to find me, shaking their heads in disbelief. One of them was on a day off but had decided to come along in her own time to support me. 'Three police officers walked out in tears during the charges,' she told Mum. 'Even the judge said it was the worst case he'd ever presided over.'

It just didn't make sense. No one knew what to do. If he'd been judged not guilty in a trial we'd have been pledging to fight back with an appeal, but now we were impotent, there was nothing we could do.

I *hated* to feel powerless; I *hated* to feel like a victim; I *hated* to feel beaten. But that's what the legal system had done to me. The courts had backed up all the negative feelings that had defined my life with Grandad.

'Four and a half years,' I muttered to myself. It sounded like a long break, not a prison sentence. It was *nothing* compared to the crimes he had committed. My anger bubbled up inside me again. Why was this happening? I had wanted to take my power back, but it had been snatched off me again. My only comfort was that I had four years to live my life free of his shadow.

But from that moment, it was as if someone had tipped an egg timer upside down. All I could do was watch helplessly as the sand slid through it, marking the time until he was released and would be free to hunt me down.

As far as the legal system was concerned, the matter was closed, but it wasn't over for me. Grandad might be serving four years, but I was the one serving a life sentence. My prison was inside me.

17. Falling Apart

After the hearing, I tried to get on with my life. Daniel had been a massive support, and we were now living together. Mum warned me I was too young to settle down, but after the life I'd led, I just needed somewhere to call home and somebody to love. It was like a fairytale to have my own house – we even had a little black and white cat. These four walls are my four walls, I'd think to myself. No one gets past that front door unless I ask them to.

Then I got some shocking news. I was pregnant. It was only a month after Grandad had been sentenced, and I was still only sixteen.

Even though Mum and Dad were worried when I broke the news, they supported my decision to keep the baby. Daniel had a good job, we had a lovely house, so things weren't as bad as they could have been.

In the short term, at least, it took my mind off Grandad. For the moment he was locked away, and I had a baby to worry about. Of course it terrified me to think about what would happen when he was released. I felt I couldn't protect myself, so how could I protect my baby? But I had to be strong and by seven months pregnant, I was deliriously happy. When the baby was born I believed I could forge a bond of pure love for the first time in my life.

But the curse I felt I was living under was about to strike again.

I was in the bath when I first noticed the blood. It curled into the water, dissolving from scarlet red to a sickly pink, staining the water. Panicking, I pulled myself out, stroking my heavily pregnant belly. As the blood ran in persistent streaks down the insides of my legs I started screaming and screaming. Daniel was working, so I was alone. Staggering to the phone, I managed to call an ambulance.

Within ten minutes I was being raced to a maternity hospital. The sound of sirens and the smell inside ambulances turned my stomach, but this time I was too worried about my baby to connect to this fear. Faces loomed over me. Kindly nurses and stern doctors prodded my belly and consulted among themselves while they did an emergency scan.

'We can't find a heartbeat,' a doctor broke the news, as a nurse held my hand, her expression oozing sympathy and concern.

Because I was seven months pregnant I still had to deliver my baby. Pumped full of so many drugs I was barely on the planet, I gave birth to a stillborn little boy. They took him away before I could even hold him. I felt a terrible hollowness creep into my heart. I'd lost everything, even my baby.

Even though my little boy had been stillborn, I had been given a bed among new mothers and that night, the sound of crying babies was like razors in my ears. I was consumed with jealousy and anger. Once again, those words punched into my mind: *Why me?* What have

I done to deserve this? It felt that the guilty weren't punished in life, only the innocent.

Lying there, still full of drugs, everything connected in my mind from the abuse, to my family falling apart and now finally to losing my baby. My heartbeat was like a fist clenching in anger. The last strong part of me snapped.

A few days later the hospital officials said they could either sign the body of my baby over to me or they would cremate him. I was completely distraught; there was no way I could cope with arranging for his burial on my own. So, blinking back the tears, I signed on the dotted line for them to lay Kieran to rest.

Back at home, I had become a different person. Emotionally, I was wired to the moon. I felt a witch had cursed me, and that nothing good would ever happen to me. Full of self-pity, I started to blame myself, figuring that my body was so damaged inside, I couldn't even carry a baby.

Nothing ever goes right in my life, I thought with bitterness.

Daniel wasn't coping well either. He couldn't be there for me in the way I needed, and our relationship became increasingly volatile. I knew I wanted out. We were tearing each other apart. My relationship with my dad had completely broken down too. He was there for the big events in my life, like the court case, but day to day we couldn't cope with each other.

We'd stopped being simply a father and daughter. I was the little girl his father had been jailed for abusing, and he was the son of the man who had destroyed my life. We defined ourselves by the abuse. After I lost Kieran, Dad and Joan had given me money so I could go and visit Mum for a few days, but beyond that, we had nothing to say to each other. We didn't hate one another or blame each other – we simply couldn't look at each other through innocent eyes. We didn't know how to reconnect our relationship. Joan didn't help either, she was still in the background, trying to steer Dad away from me. In a strange way, both Dad and I had been victims of the same people in life – we'd just been manipulated in different ways.

But now, more depressed than I ever, I felt utterly alone.

If I wanted to leave Daniel, my only option was to go to a shelter for the homeless. It seemed a drastic thing to do, but I felt I had no option.

I struggled to write a goodbye note.

'I can't take any more,' I wrote with a shaky hand. 'Since I lost the baby I can't cope any more. I have to leave.' Then, in a childish swirl I added, 'PS Don't forget to feed the cat.' It was a strange thing to worry about but I couldn't take my little cat with me, and I wanted her looked after. I was only seventeen and, although I'd been through so much, I still had a girlish attitude to life. But my youthful courage was fading fast.

Walking out of the house, I couldn't face looking back. This was my life now, and I had to accept it.

Arriving at the shelter, my heart contracted with fear as I saw the large, grey faceless building, with dozens of windows peering out like squinting eyes. It reminded me of the estate where Grandad had lived. There was the same coldness, as if it were inhospitable to any kind of happiness.

The warden showed me up to my room and explained the rules. Only married couples or single women were allowed in the shelter. You had to be back in your room by ten o'clock at night, and for the first few months you weren't allowed a key to your room. The wardens would lock your door when you left and unlock it on your return. It was a prison by another name.

The furniture was cheap and basic – like something you might find in the home of a poor old-age pensioner. The floor was covered with cheap lino and had a terrible infestation of silver fish. With harsh strip lighting and no lamps to soften the atmosphere, it felt like a clinical interrogation suite. It was certainly not a place you could call home.

I slowly unpacked my small bag of personal belongings and then sat at the cheap Formica table, holding my head in my hands. Tears streamed in rivulets through my fingers. I didn't want to think it, but I couldn't help it drifting into my mind: Grandad had been right. He had threatened that if I told my secret I would lose everything and everybody. He'd been proved right. Here I was, alone, in what amounted to an orphanage. My life was grim and loveless. I knew if I called Mum she'd come and fetch me, but I felt I'd already been a big enough burden on her. She'd warned me not to settle down too young, and I didn't want to admit that she'd been right. I started to think that everyone would be better off without me. What was the point of my life? I thought I'd reached rock bottom.

But over the next few weeks, things got even worse.

The shelter was full of people who were at best damaged or at worst dangerous. Because I didn't have a key to lock my door when I was there, thugs could burst in and take anything they wanted. A couple of women had singled me out to pick on. Once again, I felt like I had 'victim' tattooed on my forehead. Every day their bullying got worse, until one day they barged in, slapping me around, kicking me and verbally abusing me. I held my arms up to shield my face, but I was too broken to fight back. Let them do their worst, I thought. I'd stopped caring.

Grandad's evil promises were true. I'd been sent away to a hellish place where people beat me up on a regular basis. He was right.

All the emotions I hadn't dealt with over the abuse started to bubble to the surface. I felt an explosive mixture of anger at what he had done to me, combined with a growing sense of misplaced guilt. Sitting under the strip lighting, looking out of the window at the bleak gloomy skies, I tortured myself with memories, questioning every decision I had taken since childhood. 'What if I hadn't worn my short Minnie Mouse nightie in front of him?' I asked myself, searching for reasons to explain why he'd started to sexually abuse me. 'Should I have covered myself up more?' Of course this was an insane way to think – the guilt and blame were all his, not mine – but everything had started to twist round in my mind as I sank into a deeper and deeper depression.

I also felt responsible for splitting the family up. I convinced myself that it was my fault that Gran's and

Dad's lives had been ruined. I took the whole burden and packed it on my own shoulders. It wasn't logical, but I'd stopped seeing the world in a rational way.

One night I realized there was only one way out. I'd spent my whole life fighting and battling, but now I wanted to give up. I was exhausted by all the pain and suffering I'd been through. 'I'd be better off dead,' I told myself.

I wrote a note addressed to all my family, explaining that everything was my fault.

'I should never have told anyone what Grandad did to me,' I wrote in small squashed writing – I didn't even feel my words deserved to take up much space in the world. 'I've been a burden on everyone, and you'd be better off without me ...' at that thought, a sob wrenched my chest. I dropped the pen and walked calmly into the bathroom. The lino was cold under my bare feet, but I couldn't even feel it. I had gone into the place of numbness, the hole I used to fall into when Grandad abused me. I was beyond emotion. The bathroom cabinet was full of medication. Since I'd broken my silence, psychologists had prescribed tranquillizers to calm me down. I also suffered from asthma, and I had bottles and bottles of pills designed to open my airways when I was having an attack. I grabbed them all, regardless. With a glass of murky water I started to swallow them one by one, building up into handfuls, which made me gag in horror.

Before long I'd swallowed over a hundred tablets and had started to feel a blissful wooziness come over me. It was an enticing tiredness, not the hopeless fatigue

I usually felt. I lay down on the brown sofa, allowing my head to fall back on the cushion. I'd already asked the warden to give me a wake-up call in the morning, by which time they'd find me dead.

I want it to be over, I thought, feeling more peaceful than I had in many years. I could feel myself drifting away. It was similar to the feeling I had when Grandad had plied me with drugs. Only this time no one was going to hurt me, I was going somewhere safe. I could feel the wind on my face, the trees whispering, beckoning me to go deeper into the woods, everything was getting lighter, clearer . . .

A sharp slap across the face brought me round from my fatal reverie. I could see people looming over me like ominous shadows. Then I slipped back into a dream world illuminated by a brilliant light. It was like being in heaven and everything was shimmering with whiteness. But a sound started to edge it's way into the beautiful peace of the place I was in. At first it was a soft buzz but, before long, I heard a loud wailing siren. I opened my eyes and saw Ellie, a friend from the shelter, peering down at me. Behind her were men, feverishly pulling at tubes and wires.

I was in an ambulance. On instinct Ellie had popped round to check if I was okay – we'd spoken briefly that day, and she'd sensed I was really down. When she found me slumped on the sofa, she'd guessed instantly what I'd done and dialled 999.

'Stay with us,' she said urgently, 'please stay with us.'

I closed my eyes, trying to find the beautiful, white magical land I'd been travelling into. I wanted to go back there. 'Leave me alone, I want to die,' I muttered, through lips stuck together with the dryness of near death.

At the hospital, there was frantic action surrounding me. I gazed up at the white ceiling, tinged with brown damp, and was blinded by the lights.

My heart was beating a million times to the dozen, and you could actually see it heaving in my chest in clear distress. It was hard to breathe, and no matter how much I gasped, I couldn't fill my lungs. A nurse forced a tube down my throat, and then I blacked out. This time there was no light, just the deep velvety darkness of complete unconsciousness.

The next time I woke up, things were calmer. Mum was by my side, holding my hand with a harrowed look on her face. We both burst into tears.

'Thank God,' she whispered, gently kissing my face.

A doctor stood by, saying, 'We've got bad news. You're at serious risk of a heart attack.' Apparently most of the pills I'd taken had been for asthma, and in such large quantities they'd expanded my lungs to grotesque proportions, putting a terrible pressure on my heart.

For the next week they kept me in for observation. A psychologist came round to see me. He asked if I'd try to commit suicide again.

'Yes,' I told him bluntly. I hadn't succeeded, but I still wanted to die.

'Well, we'll have to keep you in here then,' he informed me.

That was my worst fear. Trapped there against my own will.

'Okay, what if I promise not to try it again?' I asked.

'Then I can sign your discharge form.'

'I won't do it again then,' I promised, lying through my teeth.

So I was released from the hospital. Mum looked after me for a while, but when I finally seemed better, she had to get on with her life. I went back to the same, scummy room at the shelter, feeling just as despairing as ever. But I couldn't try and kill myself again. The look on Mum's face had seen to that; pain was etched into it, and I couldn't put her though that another time.

Now I dealt with my pain in a different way. Remembering the relief I'd got by scrubbing my body raw after Grandad's attacks, I started self-harming. I'd break plastic cassette covers by stamping on them with the heel of my boot, then use the sharp, raggy shard of plastic to hack away at my skin until I was covered in red sores. My body was poison. This was the only way of bleeding the pain out. I was caught in a cycle of self-destructive behaviour.

After my suicide attempt, my doctor had become reluctant to prescribe me Valium any more. He said they were addictive, and that I should try and do without them. The other, unspoken, reason was that he didn't want to give me the means to make another attempt on my life. But the truth was, as he'd said, I *was* addicted to tranquillizers. I suffered terrible flashbacks from the abuse, and getting to sleep without medication was impossible. I couldn't escape the memories or the pain; I needed something to numb them.

Unable to get them legally, I decided to buy them on the black market. There were lots of drug dealers who hung round the homeless shelter and, one night, tormented by emotions I couldn't cope with, I paid one a visit.

'Aren't you the girl from the newspapers?' he asked as I walked in. His long hair hung greasily around his face, and he was puffing on a roll-up. He'd recognized me from all the local press after the trial.

I nodded, shuffling with embarrassment. I didn't want to talk about *that* in a place like *this*. I just wanted something to help me sleep.

'Are you okay?' he asked, with what seemed to be a genuine look of concern. He stubbed his cigarette out and eyed me up and down.

He'd asked the golden question. I instantly flushed, glad that someone was concerned about me, and had asked how I was feeling.

'How are you're coping?' he continued, 'you must be having some really bad dreams.'

How did he know? I thought to myself with surprise. My nightmares were awful. Every night I slipped into a deep dark slimy sleep where unknown monsters crouched in the recesses of my mind, ready to pounce.

'I'm having really bad dreams,' I admitted, looking shyly at him.

'I can help with that,' he said in a knowing tone, lighting another cigarette.

'Really?' I replied quickly, barely able to contain my relief.

'Here take this,' he pressed a lump of something into my hand, his touch lingering a bit too long.

'What is it?' I asked naively.

'Brown,' he told me, with a twitch of his lips.

I'd never heard of it, but if it got me to sleep I was happy to try it.

'It's free – after what you've been through, you deserve a good night's sleep,' he told me, explaining how I should smoke it.

He grinned, a wide, yellow-stained smile, as I happily made my way out.

Back in my own room, I looked out at the lights blinking in the dark, beacons of warmth in the coldness of the night. I wanted to go into a world where nothing mattered. I unwrapped the substance, fumbling around, not knowing what I was doing, but trying to remember his instructions.

Feeling nervous, I made a cup of tea and took my first drag.

Within seconds it was as though a warm bubble enveloped me. I felt as if a golden shield had appeared around me, protecting me from harm. I was melting into the most delicious warmth where nothing mattered.

The next morning I woke up feeling horrendous. The high from the night before had been fake. Everything I had stopped feeling caught up with me like a slap across the face. The pain I had been trying to forget hit me all at once. What had happened to me was still real. It still hurt.

One thought consumed me: I had to make that bubble last longer.

I was already hooked. I had become a heroin addict.

For almost a year I drifted in a haze of numbness, knowing that my life was spiralling out of control, but unable to get myself back together. Finally, friends stepped in to intervene, forcing me to do cold turkey. For five weeks my life was like a scene from *Trainspotting*. Sickness, cramps and fearful hallucinations consumed me. But eventually I began to feel normal again, and stronger than I had for a long time. I'd come back from the edge.

A few weeks later, walking along a street, I saw a sign saying 'victim support'. On impulse I walked in. A friendly woman brewed me a cup of tea, and led me into a cosy room to talk. Shaking, I drew a deep breath and told her I'd just come off heroin. I sketchily explained what had got me hooked in the first place, but I couldn't tell her all the details, because, once again, I found it too hard to put them into words.

'You don't even have to talk about it,' she reassured me in a gentle voice. 'We can talk about anything you want.'

So week after week I went back, drip-feeding her pieces of my story. I still couldn't fully explain – I thought she'd be too disgusted. Instead, she asked me to keep a diary, noting down any words that popped into my mind or felt significant.

On one visit I tentatively pushed the pages towards her. 'Lollipop,' she read out slowly. She began quizzing me and, as the real meaning came tumbling out, I tried to hold back my tears. I'd spent years blocking it out.

From then on, she encouraged me to write down my feelings. I started to put every emotion I felt down on paper, often in the form of poetry.

Sometimes I'd feel so disgusted by what I'd written I

couldn't bring myself to show it to her. She'd hand me a match. Right there in the room, I'd set it alight and watch it burn, disintegrating into nothing.

'It doesn't matter if no one reads it,' she explained, 'it's getting it out from inside you that counts.'

I'd also started attending counselling sessions at a rehab centre. They explained that I had a right to grieve for the little girl Grandad had taken from me. It was okay to feel sad or angry. Gradually, I realized that I was letting the abuse define me. It was shaping every decision about my life. I was letting Grandad win.

I started to think about my dad. We both loved each other so much – it was crazy to let the abuse ruin our relationship. I decided to write him a letter.

I told him how important he was to me, and that we needed to start treating each other with respect. I said he had to reply in seven days or consider me dead to him. It was now or never to rebuild the trust between us. Eight days later I got a heartfelt letter. Thanks to Royal Mail, it was a day late, so when it arrived in the post I burst into tears. I had thought he didn't care.

'I love you so much,' he'd written in bold, manly print. 'I don't want to lose you, Emily, you mean the world to me.'

When we spoke on the phone later, we could barely understand each other in between the emotional sobs and happy tears we were both crying.

He'd also split up from Joan, which was a massive relief. He'd finally seen through her, realizing what a mean person she was. 'I'll never forgive myself,' he told me, crying so much I could hardly believe it was the same repressed father I'd always known, who didn't like to discuss feelings.

A few weeks later we had an emotional reunion. To make amends, he set me up in a new flat, which was bright, clean and cheerful.

Things were finally coming together for me.

But as always, Grandad had other plans.

Just before I turned twenty-one, I got a letter from the police advising me that my grandfather was about to be released from prison. The egg timer had just run out. My legs turned to jelly, and for a moment I considered turning to the only thing that had ever blocked out the memories of what he'd done: heroin. Then the survivor in me kicked back.

'Do I lose my family again, or do I start fighting back?' I asked myself, feeling strength flood into me. I'm going to fight.

I was scared that he would be walking the streets again, but I vowed to not let that thought stop me living my life.

I refuse to let him have that power over me any more.

18. Finding Happiness

After years of being lost, I finally started to find myself. I had my own flat, and I was determined to stand on my own two feet. My life had been defined by the actions of other people – now I wanted to define myself.

Walking past a local newsagent I saw a small hand-written advertisement, saying, 'Singer Wanted'. I paused for a moment, thinking, No, I couldn't, but something pulled me towards it and before I knew it, I had written the number down. I'd been singing all my life and it was the one thing I truly loved. It was a way for me to express myself, which made me feel safe.

But singing in front of an audience was another matter altogether. I was still very self-conscious, so the thought of standing on a stage terrified me. The fighter in me wanted to bring it on. 'You're frightened of it? Okay then, that's what we'll do.' I wanted to push against my limits.

I auditioned and miraculously got the job. I was now a professional singer. The other band members were five men. I should have felt threatened by that, but I didn't. They were so protective, especially once they knew what I'd been through. We toured all over the place, often sharing bedrooms together. They were like my big brothers and they restored my faith in men.

My first professional gig was absolutely nerve wracking.

It was only to a crowd of about thirty people in a local pub, but it felt like performing at Wembley Arena. It was a special occasion because my dad and Tom had come down to support me, and I could see their smiling faces, wishing me well, but also nervous on my behalf. I went on stage, covered head to foot – I couldn't bear to show any part of my body to begin with – to a roar from the crowd, and started to sing the first few lines of 'Dignity' by Deacon Blue, stumbling over the words. Suddenly I raced off stage, rushed to the toilets and threw up

I felt *so* humiliated. Looking into the mirror, I blinked at my reflection, barely recognizing the pretty girl with black kohl round her eyes looking back. I can't go back out there, I told myself, trembling. Imagining Dad's worried face, my inner strength kicked back in. If I could face Grandad in court, I could certainly face going back on stage. I strutted back, grabbed the microphone and a huge round of applause engulfed the room. I could see Dad and Tom clapping wildly.

When I got to the last verse, I looked into the audience and saw tears streaming down my father's face. The look of pride and love in his eyes will stay with me for ever.

For years I'd been ashamed of myself, now I felt proud to be me.

Over the next few years, my confidence grew. Singing became my counselling. I started to dress more sexily, exploring my female power and enjoying it. On stage I jumped around, wore gorgeous outfits and sang my heart out. It felt good to show such a positive side of me. I was finding a new way to express myself, realizing that I had control. Men could look at me, but that was all they could do without my permission. It was liberating.

Soon, we were performing in front of much bigger audiences.

The best moment was playing to over 2,000 people at a televised sports event. Knowing my nerves, the boys in the band didn't tell me how big it was until the moment I got on stage. I'd already spent hours and hours getting ready. I'd curled my long blonde hair into ringlets, and carefully applied my make-up, just as I'd watched Mum do when I was a little girl.

It's impossible to see the audience when the lights are out on a big stage. I walked on in darkness, hearing a hub of noise that surprised me with its volume. My heart was beating and my hands were trembling so much I could barely hold the microphone. A spotlight beamed on the guitarist as he struck up the first chords, then a second spotlight picked out the keyboard player. Then boom: three spotlights hit me at once and I knew that in a few seconds I would have to start singing. But for the first time, I *saw* the size of the crowd. I could see band members looking at each other, thinking: Will she run off? For a moment, as always, I froze. I wasn't sure the words would come out of my mouth. But on cue, I found myself singing the Eurythmics' 'Sweet Dreams (Are Made of This)' as the crowd erupted into a massive cheer.

I felt my own power. It wasn't just a special night because of the sheer scale of it – I was also performing a very special song. Annie Lennox had been my hero all through my childhood. Hers were the songs I'd sung into a hairbrush, trying to escape the reality of what was happening to me. I knew all the lyrics off by heart, and they really spoke to me. As I got older their meanings clicked with me more and more. They were about protecting yourself while freeing yourself at the same time – and helping others to do the same. Standing on stage, singing the lyrics Annie Lennox had stood on stage and sung, felt surreal. Punching my hands in the air, I felt sexy, confident and totally empowered.

I'm not going to let *anyone* knock me down again, I thought to myself as the lights glittered, and the shapes of hundreds of faces formed in front of me, cheering me on, not judging me on anything but the present moment.

As I reached the lyrics that meant the most to me, I could feel my heart race, and as I sung the final words, it felt incredibly poignant.

When I first heard the song, I'd been outraged by the last line, implying that some people would actually *want* to be abused. But as I'd got older, I'd begun to understand the implications of this lyric. I'd come to realize that if you've been abused, you end up taking it out on other people or yourself. Often you're *not* empowered, you're in victim mode. People take advantage of that to abuse you even further. Sometimes, you even abuse yourself. In my case, to stop the pain, I'd turned to self-harming, then to heroin.

If addiction of any kind grips your life, you're still handing power to your abuser. They're still destroying your life. You're *allowing* them to destroy your life. You have to take your power back, and fight against everything they'd want you to become.

On my personal journey, I'd learned that the most important thing is to respect yourself, your own body and your feelings. Often, your own feelings will be the most terrifying thing in the world, but you have to face them. Doctors want to prescribe tablets, but the best medication is to talk. When we speak out, abusers lose their power. Then victims become survivors.

'Sweet Dreams' became an anthem of empowerment to me and, right then and there on stage, I vowed to keep on fighting, for myself – and others.

Of course, this is a constantly evolving process. No one gets there straight away, and it's always an ongoing battle.

When I was twenty-three I met my husband, Andy, who was older than me. We got married for all the wrong reasons. He made me feel safe and secure, and really looked after me, and I thought that was what I wanted. It was emotional security with someone who was my best friend, but not love in the romantic sense. But at first we were happy and determined to have a baby together. By the time I was twenty-seven, after three miscarriages, I finally heard the news I'd been desperate to hear – I was pregnant.

But my delight was also laced with fear when I found out I was expecting a little girl.

My grandad's evil words still swirled in my mind.

'If you have a daughter, I'll teach her to become a woman too . . .'

If *I* hadn't been safe how could I ever protect a little girl of my own? How could I guarantee she wouldn't have her life shattered too?

As the baby grew in my belly, I bloomed. This was the first moment of feeling truly alive I'd had for years. I'd spent my whole life wearing different masks to disguise how something had died inside me the first time my grandad had touched me. With my own baby on the way I felt part of me had finally been given back – the bit that wasn't tainted by him. If anyone hurts my baby I'll kill them! I thought to myself fiercely, stroking my swollen tummy protectively.

The pregnancy was a tough one. I kept bleeding constantly and doctors warned me that I might lose the baby. I'd already had three miscarriages, as well as my stillborn baby, Kieran. The doctors confirmed that my difficulty carrying a baby to term was probably due to the internal injuries I'd sustained from my grandad's abuse. Even now my body was still a battleground. But I was determined finally to hold my own baby in my arms.

The next few months were touch and go for the baby. This little girl, with so much hanging over her head already, was struggling to find her way into the world. Then the worst possible news came. I'd been at the hospital having a routine scan, when the nurse's words shattered my blossoming happiness.

'I'm afraid we can't see the baby's heartbeat any more,'

she said, her voice drifting off softly, as we all looked at the screen.

We were nearly there, I thought, tears streaming down my face. This couldn't be happening. I slumped in my chair, as if the energy had been vacuumed out of me. After everything I'd been through, I was going to lose this baby too – the little girl I'd already fallen in love with. A silent howl screamed inside my head. This baby was *meant* to be, I sobbed to myself, clutching my swollen stomach.

The nurse touched me gently on the shoulder and said they would prepare for an emergency operation. I knew what that meant.

As I was being wheeled down the grey, windowless corridors to the theatre I was gripped by a sudden knowing. It was pure mother's intuition.

'Turn back,' I suddenly demanded. 'I want another scan. I need to be sure my baby isn't still alive before I do this.'

I didn't know where my inner strength came from.

I could see the nurses exchange pitying looks. They thought it was a waste of time, and that I was hysterical. But they obviously felt sorry for me and turned the trolley round, heading back to the scanning room.

As the machine switched on, the thud of a tiny heartbeat suddenly sounded through the silence, reverberating round the consultation room in a deafening rhythm. The medical staff gulped, knowing what they had been about to do.

The baby was still alive.

With every beat on that monitor, something inside

me got stronger and stronger. I'd always wanted to be a mum, but this feeling blew me away.

At first everyone was in shock, but then the room erupted in cheers.

I hugged Andy, sobbing with relief. I was too happy to be angry with the doctors over their mistake at this point.

'There's something special about this one,' I said, stroking my tummy, tears of relief streaming down my face.

Six months later Sophie was born.

As she came into the world, Mum squeezed my hand tightly. I felt overwhelmed by the knowledge that there were three generations in that room. It felt as though me and Mum were really bonding and passing on the torch to the next generation, vowing not to make the same mistakes.

'Her eyes are opening,' my mum whispered to me with wonder and awe.

Still attached to the umbilical chord, the doctor passed my beautiful baby to me and straight away Sophie started breastfeeding, her tiny body resting on my chest. I realized that having a baby girl was a gift – a way to put things right. It was another step in my healing process.

As the years passed, my marriage became increasingly rocky. I realized I needed to protect *myself*, not look to other people for safety. Andy wanted to take care of me, but that made me feel like a little girl again. I wanted to take charge in a positive way, and become a woman in the truest sense of the word. I wanted power for myself.

In 2006, when I was twenty-nine, we separated

amicably, and are still the best of friends. Our main priority has always been Sophie's happiness.

Wanting to invest in myself, I went back to college. Despite having dyslexia, I gained a diploma in holistic therapy, completed my first-year diploma in psychology, a national certificate in social care and in health care, health promotion and equal opportunities. My qualifications were all about helping other people and not just myself. After what I've been through, I know how bad life can get and how much help people need to get through it.

But the real gift in my life is my daughter, Sophie. Grandad always said I was tainted. He was wrong. I've created the most perfect, beautiful little girl. That innocence came from inside me. No matter how he damaged my body, and despite the babies I lost because of that damage, this baby survived. Like me, she's a fighter. Together we are so strong. I can see the world through her innocent eyes. I can never get my childhood back, but I can feel pure through my little girl.

Grandad also said I'd lose my family. He was wrong. Mum, Dad, my three brothers and I are closer than ever. Now we have children of our own to keep our family name going, as something we can be proud of and protect.

As the circle of time turns, life has brought me back to the small sleepy village I lived in with my father at the police house. On windswept mornings, with icy blue skies and the salty smell of sea breezes, Sophie and I head out to the woods to walk the same paths I walked as a child. Lassie is long gone, but we walk past the spot where her ashes are scattered, with Sophie pleading for a dog of her own. Like me, she has a big imagination to go with her personality. She also has the same sense of magic about the world. When twigs break underfoot, she'll stop with a jolt and whisper, 'Mummy, it's goblins walking through the woods!' As we pass secluded alcoves where I would huddle up for safety, crying silent tears, she'll knock on trees and wait for the fairies to answer back. She's convinced they're hiding in there, behind a magic doorway. Now she's the one telling the stories. The difference is she's creating a magical fantasy world for fun, not to escape from a life of horror and abuse. There is no frightening villain in her fairyland, preying on the shadows of her childish innocence.

We walk past the Witch's Castle, and she looks up in wonder saying, 'I think a princess belongs here.' I nod in agreement, a sad smile on my face.

When she'd old enough, her inheritance will be my story. As a mother I want to protect her from the worst details, but I also want her to know the truth. I'm saving a copy of this book in a carved, wooden treasure chest for her to open when the time is right.

I want Sophie to grow up to become a strong, beautiful, independent woman, who knows her own value and understands that there are no secrets that need to be kept in this world. Silence is poison. Sharing our stories will bring us together and make us strong. We need to protect the next generation. They are the ones who will build the future. If we fail them, we fail everyone.

My grandad is still alive, still walking the streets, still free to abuse other children. People often wonder why I don't hunt him down for revenge.

'I don't want to sink to his level,' I tell them. Violence is not the answer. I don't want to go after Grandad to make him suffer the physical pain he inflicted on me – I just want justice, to challenge the system and make sure this never happens to my daughter or anyone else's child, ever again. We have to save the next generation.

We have to say these words, believe them and *make* them happen: *the cycle ends here.*

Acknowledgements

So much of my childhood was spent being the keeper of a secret I was too terrified to share. After spending so many years with that burden, I would now like to thank everyone who helped me break my silence.

It was the love and support of my big brother that first helped me speak out. Thank you for asking the right questions, and for believing in me. You gave me back my life and helped me breathe again.

I also want to thank my mum and dad for believing in me and supporting me. You both gave me the inspiration and strength to be the person I am. You helped me on my path from victim to survivor. Because of you I have the courage to strive to be the best person I can for myself and for my daughter.

To my two other brothers, I thank you for supporting me and never judging my choices during my journey to becoming a survivor. You have both been there for me unconditionally, and I will always be grateful for that.

I would also like to thank my primary school teacher for encouraging me – you gave me the inspiration in my darkest times to follow my dreams and pursue music. I will always be grateful to you and the rest of my teachers.

I would also like to say thank you to Annie Lennox, through her music and lyrics I found a way to understand myself. Growing up, she was a role model to me, as a woman full of strength and courage.

To those true and trusted friends that have supported me over the years, I thank you for being there for me in the good times and the bad.

And last but by no means least I have to say a massive thank you to my three musketeers, without them I would never have been able to tell my story.

To my agent Susan Smith for always guiding me in the right direction – you have always been so supportive and I am glad to call you a friend.

To my editor Paulette Hearn for her faith in my story – and her determination that it was a story that needed to be told.

And to Amanda Astill, without you it would not be possible. You gave me the courage to tell my story. You helped me find my voice. For that I thank you, you are part of my heart and family.

There are also people who would rather I had not told my story. They find it hard to understand why I would want to write about these events. So I also acknowledge them by saying – I do it because I refuse to be a keeper of secrets any more.

The shame and guilt of what happened belongs to one person – my grandfather. I hope that by telling my story it will educate people about what goes on behind closed doors. If this book helps at least one person break their silence, then it will be a step towards changing our attitudes, and protecting our future generations.

My final acknowledgement is to all survivors of abuse:

May you find your path to breaking your own silence. And please never stop fighting, never give up.